"This book is filled with two of my favorite things: unrepentant 80s nostalgia and unbridled geek pop culture obsession. If you're not already a fan, Richter will make you one. And if you already love Duran Duran, this book will make you love and appreciate them even more."

—Ernest Cline, author of READY PLAYER ONE

DURANALYSIS

essays on the duran duran experience

morgan richter

To all the Duranies.
Past, present, and future.

CONTENTS

INTRODUCTION

IT'S 1983, AND I'm spending the night at my friend Kara's house. Kara, like me, is nine years old; her sister Katie is a couple of years younger. We're the only ones here. Kara's parents will be out late at some event, and instead of hiring a babysitter to watch their two small children, they've opted to add another small child to the mix. In the eighties, this was considered a totally sensible and appropriate approach to parenting, and one my own parents enthusiastically endorsed. Kara lives down the block from me; she has a swimming pool and cable television, complete with all the *good* channels, so hanging out at her place is always an excellent idea. She also owns an Intellivision gaming console. We kick the evening off with some *Advanced Dungeons & Dragons: Cloudy Mountain*.

We play for far too long. The console overheats, and the game goes wonky. Dragons drift through solid stone and slide through walls instead of sticking to the dungeon corridors. This is likely a feature, not a glitch, but my hyperactive imagination chooses to interpret this as something supernatural, like the boundaries of the game are threatening to erode, unleashing dangerous magic into the physical world.

We settle in for some quality time with premium cable. We have plans to watch *Star Wars,* but we somehow grievously misinterpret the *TV Guide* listings, because—whoops!—HBO seems to be showing *Barbarella* instead. We've promised Kara's parents we won't watch any R-rated movies, but *Barbarella* looks like a safe bet. It's bright and colorful and cheerful, filled with bouncy music and pretty women with shiny hair. It's fine for kids, probably.

Early on in our viewing, long before the evil scientist Durand-Durand locks the titular heroine into a contraption designed to kill her by exhausting her through an endless series of powerful orgasms, we've grown wise to the idea that this is probably not a film Kara's parents would be thrilled about us seeing. We're committed, though—frankly, we are *riveted*—and we watch it to the end. (We then follow it up with a viewing of the violent and sleazy animated sci-fi anthology *Heavy Metal.* We see a whole lot of breasts that night, I'm just saying. In for a penny, in for a pound.)

Later that week, my sister and I go for a hike in our neighborhood. We live on the western edge of Spokane, in a log cabin built on the top of a hill with a panoramic view of peaks and valleys. Our backyard is littered with large volcanic rock formations anchored by a huge dark sphere maybe twelve feet tall, which serves as a nifty Death Star in many a Star Wars-centric playtime scenario. Just past the rock barrier is a sloping hillside covered with long-needled Ponderosa pine trees. The swiftest and best way to get to the bottom of the hill is to sit on a piece of cardboard and slide down the thick blanket of fallen needles.

At the base of the hill, there's a trail and a decision to be made. Head right, and we'll find ourselves in a tangled grove of lilac trees growing wild in the middle of nowhere. Head left, and the trail abruptly ends at a shallow cement chasm, which is part of Spokane's abandoned trolley line, out of service since 1936. We go left, then jump down into the chasm. We find ourselves facing a wall covered with graffiti, the work of local hoodlums and/or bored artisans. I stare at words emblazoned on concrete in foot-high spray-painted letters: *Duran Duran.*

My brain makes the connection, as random and improbable as it seems. "That's from the weird movie I watched with Kara," I tell my sister. Three years older and infinitely more clued in to the pop culture of the day, my sister replies with appropriate scorn: "They're a *band.*"

Duran Duran are a band. Duran Duran have been famous for two years already, but this is the first I've heard of them, and now things will never be the same.

Knowing about Duran Duran unlocks a new level in my mind. The world becomes wild and weird. The dragons are now free to roam around my brain instead of sticking to pre-approved neurological pathways. Now that I'm aware of their existence, Duran Duran are *everywhere* in Spokane in 1983. For the first time, I start listening to pop music on the local radio station instead of sticking to our parents' collection of show tunes and folk albums. We don't have MTV, and opportunities to see Duran Duran's amazing, iconic music videos are few and far between, so whenever I happen to catch one— maybe at Kara's house, maybe while watching *Friday Night Videos* on NBC—my brain kicks into a higher gear, trying to absorb and memorize every baffling detail. The secrets of the universe can be found in the "Union of the Snake" video, I'm pretty sure, if I could only view it enough times to unravel them.

(From my vantage point here in 2017, I'm still half-convinced the secrets of the universe can be found in the "Union of the Snake" video.)

We're all going Duran-mad at my elementary school, even though we fall outside Duran Duran's peak demographic, which is comprised of teens and twentysomethings. The band members themselves seem preposterously sophisticated and glamorous; they all have beautiful girlfriends, or maybe they're all married—the teen magazines are a little coy with the details of their personal lives. They're so far out of my league as to barely register as actual human beings. They are Celebrities with an uppercase C, as exotic and strange as aliens, or androids, or exquisitely lovely demons.

I trade my Social Studies notes to a classmate for a handful of pinups of the band members. At the grocery store, I pore over teen magazines—*Tiger Beat, Bop!, 16*—and scrutinize glossy photos of those pretty, pretty boys. I'm joined at the magazine rack by Sarah, a girl at my school who possesses that rare grade-school trifecta of being pretty and popular and also genuinely nice; we bond over our love of the band. She asks me who's my favorite. John Taylor, I answer, because I know the correct answer to that question is supposed to be John. Then I point at a photo of Nick Rhodes, because he's the loveliest, and because in 1983, John and Nick really *do* look a great deal alike. Sarah corrects me gently, but I've already exposed myself as a shameless Duran poseur.

(Thanks to my website, I've earned a reputation as a Duran Duran expert, but I still feel like a poseur with alarming regularity. On Twitter, I'm friends with a cluster of lifelong Duran Duran fans—Duranies—who live and breathe everything related to the band. Trying to decipher their tweets about deep cuts and night versions is like trying to puzzle out phrases in a foreign language. If I ever find myself in the happy situation of making idle small talk with Nick Rhodes at a cocktail party—suggested conversation topics: pop music from the former Yugoslavia, Buñuel versus Cocteau, the proper ranking of vegan meat substitutes, the history and ideology of vampirism, the limitations of postmodernism, and favorite shoe designers—and the discussion drifts to, say, little-known Duran Duran B-sides, I'll be revealed as a fraud in seconds.)

We're poor, which is a boulder in my path on the quest to understand All Things Duran. Someone gives me the *Rio* album on cassette tape; I buy 45 RPM singles of "Save a Prayer" and "A View to a Kill" at Pay 'n Save with money earned sweeping floors at a rehab clinic run by a family friend. This is the entirety of my Duran Duran collection. In these pre-internet days, there are huge, jagged gaps in my Duran knowledge. Terrified of being exposed, I bluff my way through conversations with hardcore fans, often with catastrophic results. When a cute boy (Nick—*of course* his name is Nick) challenges me to list all the Duran Duran songs I know, I commit a tremendous blunder by naming "Seven and the Ragged Tiger." As any self-respecting Duranie would know, that's the title of an album, not a song.

Thirty years later, I meet up with Nick in New York. A wanderer by trade, he's just arrived from Turks and Caicos; he's in the city on a layover before heading to Thailand. We meet on a street corner in Harlem on an icy winter's day, then duck into a Senegalese restaurant, chosen at random, to warm up over plates of stewed chicken and rice. I haven't seen him since his family moved from Spokane in the mid-eighties, though we're friends on Facebook. We catch each other up on our adult lives, then the discussion shifts to my website. "What's the deal with you and Duran Duran?" he asks.

Excellent question, Nick.

In seventh grade, I befriend a battle-hardened Duranie, Sherry. It's now 1985, and the Golden Age of Duran Duran is showing the first signs of instability. Sherry gives me copies of all her albums dubbed off onto cassettes in a primitive version of illegal file sharing. Sherry owns a synthesizer, and I fancy myself a singer, so we briefly form a Duran-inspired band. We call ourselves Kai Toi, which we think sounds appropriately cool and enigmatic. We spend long hours designing our logo and bare minutes rehearsing. I write us a couple of songs. Sample lyric: *You drive your black Corvette, your shoes are Adidas/I don't know why I pursue you, I know I don't need ya.* Somewhere across the Atlantic, Simon Le Bon does not feel especially threatened by my lyrical prowess.

Duran Duran tour the United States on multiple occasions throughout the eighties, successfully managing to avoid going anywhere near Spokane each time. They're not alone in this; the only concert I see during these formative years is Wang Chung. I slather my locks in Clairol Pazazz mousse in Touch of Rose, which turns my hair the color of canned tuna, and bop around with my friends to "Everybody Have Fun Tonight" until the adults seated behind us yell at us to sit down and keep still, because in Spokane in 1986, it's a breach of unwritten concert etiquette to stand up and dance. During a 2016 vacation to the Seattle area, I visit Duran Duran archivist Andrew Golub, better known in the Duran fandom as Durandy, and view his famed collection of memorabilia. While interviewing me for a prospective documentary about the fandom, he asks me on camera when I saw my first Duran Duran concert. 2011, I tell him cheerfully.

In 1991, my high school graduating class votes me Most Intelligent, probably because I'd spent the past four years yammering on to everyone within earshot about how very, very smart I was. At our twenty-year reunion, my classmates finally get it right and vote me Most Likely to Still Listen to Duran Duran.

What's the deal with you and Duran Duran? Part of it is simple nostalgia. Listening to Duran Duran takes me back to childhood, when my parents were still alive and I lived in a house with a backyard that served as a portal to adventure, when all the promise of the world lay before me, unspoiled and new. More, though, it's because Duran Duran formed me in some hard to define way, as though Simon, Nick, John, Roger, and Andy stuck their well-moisturized and artfully manicured fingers into every part of my psyche. Through Duran Duran, I learned that substance can be found within style, that apocalyptic wastelands are easier to face when armed with a healthy dose of sparkle and brio, that tailored silk suits in candy colors are appropriate yachting attire, that the mundane and the surreal are frequent bedfellows, that wild boys always shine.

What's the deal with me and Duran Duran? Read on; I'll tell you.

CHAPTER ONE: JUST AN ART SCHOOL PUNK BAND

THE DURAN DURAN origin story begins in Birmingham, England in the late 1970s, when the UK was in the grip of a dire economic recession that would worsen and deepen as the decade rolled on. Businesses failed, factories closed, unemployment soared, and the class divide widened. Deprived of opportunities, frustration and bitterness mounted among working-class youth. Bleak, angry times call for bleak, angry music, and in this volatile climate, punk rock flourished.

The Sex Pistols, formed in London in 1976, howled for anarchy in the UK. The Clash, formed in London in 1977, voiced dark fears of looming civil war. Discharge, formed in Stoke-on-Trent in 1977, called for fighting corrupt systems. The Exploited, formed in Edinburgh in 1979, protested the dearth of prospects for a better future.

DURANALYSIS

Duran Duran, formed in Birmingham in 1978, sang about cherry ice cream smiles and paradisiacal one-night stands. And they sang this while looking fabulous in pastel silk and cavorting with leggy models on yachts, or while strolling on white beaches under violet skies in far-off lands.

The punk crowd despised them. Go figure.

By all rights, Duran Duran should never have had the chance to cavort on that yacht, should never have strolled on that far-off beach. Like their punk-loving peers, they were young, undereducated, unemployable, on the dole. They were from *Birmingham*, for crying out loud, England's Detroit, an industry town where the industry had collapsed, leaving behind empty gray factories under colorless skies. Working-class kids from 1970s Birmingham didn't end up on yachts. They didn't date models, they didn't play sold-out gigs at Madison Square Garden, they didn't become household names.

Unless you're talking about Duran Duran, that is. When it comes to Duran, the usual rules are null and void.

Very few childhood photos of Nicholas James Bates—at some early point in his music career, he'll deem his surname insufficiently glamorous and switch it to "Rhodes"—exist in the public realm, probably by design. Only one can be easily found online, a posed class picture taken when Nick was maybe nine or ten. He's dressed in a plain shirt and tie; his hair is indifferently styled in a choppy bowl cut. Its existence is something of a disappointment, as it suggests that Nick Rhodes, enduring fashion icon and magnificent weirdo, is a flesh-and-blood human of mortal birth, that he didn't spring from the head of Zeus fully formed, clad from head to toe in Vivienne Westwood with a champagne flute clutched in one elegant hand and a droll *bon mot* on his expertly painted lips.

Travel back in time forty-odd years to talk to the kid in the photo. Tell him his future: Just a few short years from now, Nick, you'll form a band. The odds of success will be so slight as to be statistically insignificant, but you, kid, you'll make it big. You and your bandmates will be household names before you're out of your teens. You'll be rich, you'll be famous, and you'll be very, very beautiful. Girls will scream at the sight of you. You'll hobnob with world-renowned artists and royalty. You'll marry a model; your wedding reception will teem with live flamingos, which will perfectly match the color of: a) your tuxedo, and b) your lipstick.

Tell young Nick all this, and he'll smile beatifically at you, tolerant yet faintly bored: Yes, of course all this will happen; now tell me something I don't know.

Nick was born knowing he'd become a star. Call it prognostication via supreme self-confidence: Nick can see the future, because he knows he can rearrange the world to suit his needs through sheer force of will. It's a neat trick, but then again, there's a little bit of magic clinging to all the Durans.

Nick Rhodes grew up just outside Birmingham in the improbably-named community of Hollywood, a comfortable suburb of an uncomfortable city. *Comfortable* is a key word here: Nick, an indifferent student with a machete-sharp brain and an insatiable thirst for pop culture, was the much-loved only child of well-off working-class parents. A degree of financial security meant he had a safety net in place when he left school at sixteen to form a band with his closest friend, an older boy named Nigel Taylor. Nick's parents gave him two years to make it big before they'd cut off their support.

Didn't matter. As it turned out, no safety net was necessary. Quitting school to start a band worked out pretty well for Nick.

Two years Nick's senior, Nigel was an art student at the local polytechnic. They'd been inseparable since adolescence, bonding over their love of music: punk, funk, disco, rock, any of it and all of it. Inspired by their androgynous glam-rock heroes—Bowie was a perennial favorite—they experimented with makeup and raided their mothers' closets for blouses and coats. Nick had a synthesizer, which he'd been teaching himself to play; Nigel knew a couple of guitar chords. Forming a band seemed like a logical course of action.

Somewhere along the line, probably around the time Nick adopted Rhodes, Nigel started going by his middle name, John. Thus his metamorphosis began: While Nigel Taylor had been a sensitive, bespectacled Dada enthusiast, John Taylor was a leggy dreamboat, a once-in-a-lifetime beauty with lethal cheekbones and a magnificent shock of glossy hair that always seemed to be tumbling into his long-lashed eyes. When Duran Duran burst onto the global stage, love-struck fans would sell the world for him.

With their band still in the embryotic stage, Nick and John happened to catch Roger Vadim's *Barbarella* when it aired on British television. The film, a 1968 French-Italian coproduction, stars a big-haired, doe-eyed Jane Fonda as an intrepid space explorer in shiny satin hotpants and matching knee boots who crosses the galaxy in search of a missing scientist, Dr. Durand-Durand. (Of Duran Duran's namesake, John would write in his 2012 memoir with the faintly exhausted air of a man who's spent over half his life explaining why his band's name contains a typo, "[Y]ou can't hear the final D in the film, nor the hyphen, and there was no imbd.com back then.")[1] Nonstop sexcapades ensue. Composed of equal parts joyously sleazy camp and brain-embossing nightmare fodder, *Barbarella* is evocative, memorable, and utterly ridiculous. No wonder Nick and John gravitated toward it.

Chaos theory tells us that small changes have big effects: A butterfly flaps its wings, and a hurricane kicks up halfway around the world. Two horny English teens watch a softcore space romp for a peek at Jane Fonda's breasts, and the music world trembles from the long-lasting repercussions. Without that *Barbarella* viewing, there'd be no Duran Duran as we know it. Throughout a long and prolific career, the band has drawn artistic inspiration from a vast and varied array of sources— William S. Burroughs novels, Jean Cocteau films, Helmut Newton photos, M.C. Escher prints—but the DNA of *Barbarella* runs deepest. The film handed John and Nick a blueprint for their band's future visual style. Like *Barbarella*, Duran Duran would be bubbly and colorful and highly decorative. It would feature an angst-free and cheerfully lurid approach to sex. It'd be pretentious, nonsensical, surreal, preposterous, decadent, and hilarious, all at once.

The lead singer of their nascent band was one of John's classmates, an elegant young punk named Stephen Duffy, who wrote artsy lyrics invoking Kerouac and Fitzgerald and who'd later achieve critical respect and a modest degree of fame with both Tin Tin and the Lilac Time. With Duffy as their frontman, Duran Duran performed in punk clubs around Birmingham. It was an uneasy match. As much as Nick and John had embraced punk's DIY we-don't-know-what-we're-doing-but-hey-let's-form-a-band-anyway spirit, the label never fit. Duran Duran's ever-evolving synth-heavy sound aligned them closer to new wave, a then-emerging punk offshoot. They were champions of escapism, not gritty realism. They preferred frilly blouses and draped scarves to ripped t-shirts and leather, they liked wearing makeup, they adored glamour. They'd composed a handful of catchy songs by this point, one of which extolled the virtues of Birmingham's Rackhams department store ("Big Store"). Word to the wise: If your band's signature tune is a paean to shopping in high-end stores, your punk cred is in danger.

John abandoned the guitar in favor of playing bass. New members came and went, names only the most fervent fan would now associate with the band: Alan Curtis on guitar, Simon Colley on clarinet. Stephen Duffy stayed with Duran Duran for a year, then left to join a better band. He was replaced, briefly, by Andy Wickett, who co-wrote "Girls on Film" and signed over his rights for £600 only to watch it become a much-loved hit.

The band needed a drummer, and along came Roger Taylor—no relation to John—who'd played in punk bands around the city. A Birmingham native, Roger was quiet, competent, and easygoing. Not of least importance, he had puppy-dog eyes, great hair, and an upper torso sculpted through hours of pounding the skins. He looked good in leather; he looked equally good in poet shirts and eyeliner. Perfect Duran bait, in other words. No fools, John and Nick leapt at the chance to add him to the team.

Onward, upward. Tired of dodging the bottles hurled at them during performances, Duran Duran ditched the punk clubs and went upscale, landing a plum gig as the house band at the Rum Runner, a sleek nightclub operated by brothers Paul and Michael Berrow. Modeled after New York's legendary Studio 54, the Rum Runner was late-seventies glamour incarnate, all mirrored walls and dark leather booths and leafy palm fronds. The Berrows began managing the band, fixing them up with dedicated rehearsal space and giving them ample opportunities to gain performance experience.

Andy Taylor—no relation to John, no relation to Roger—first crossed paths with Duran Duran when he responded to the band's want ad in a trade magazine searching for a guitarist. He showed up to his audition in overalls and cowboy boots, which, for fashion-obsessed Duran Duran, was a sartorial misstep on a calamitous level, akin to auditioning for the Sex Pistols in houndstooth and spats. Andy came from a tiny fishing village up north in Newcastle; his childhood had been rough and spare, with an absent mother and not much in the way of creature comforts. At nineteen, the same age as John and Roger, Andy had been working professionally as a guitarist in a touring cover band for three years. Quick-witted, unpolished, and bristly, he was more rock-and-roll than new wave, but he was a fiend on a guitar, and he was willing to paint his face and dye his hair for the sake of band unity. Duran

Duran liked him, and more to the point, they *needed* him.

Newly jam-packed with a surfeit of unrelated dudes named Taylor, the band still lacked a frontman. Enter Simon Le Bon, a tall and preposterously handsome vision in skintight pink leopard-skin trousers. A few years older than the other Durans, he was a drama major at Birmingham University; he'd been raised in the London suburbs, where he'd performed in local theater and television commercials as a child. He could sing, and he had a knack for writing strange and inscrutable lyrics. Bursting at the seams with confidence and bravado, Simon had the soul of a poet and the ego of a rock star, a combination that eventually helped turn him into one of the UK's most irresistible commodities, right up there with Welsh corgis, minted lamb pasties, and umbrellas emblazoned with the Union Jack.

Take a look at *Sing Street,* John Carney's 2016 film about a group of working-class teens in 1985 Dublin who try to escape their grim, dead-end lives by forming a Duran Duran-inspired new wave band (the film, a shameless valentine to Duran Duran, contains a scene in which characters sit around watching the band's iconic "Rio" video while gushing about how John Taylor is beautiful and talented; this sort of thing could seem insufferably sycophantic, but John Taylor really *is* beautiful and talented, so it works). The film ends—hey, spoiler alert!—with the young protagonist sneaking out of his home in the middle of the night and, with his girlfriend and his demo tape in tow, heading off to London in the hopes of making it big. It's a jubilant moment that turns melancholy on reflection: He has no money, no prospects, no connections, no reasonable chance of success. He's not going to make it.

Duran Duran, though. Duran Duran made it. Duran Duran *crushed* it.

If they'd never made it past the Rum Runner, well, that wouldn't have been such a bad end. They would've been doing what they loved at the poshest club in the city, playing their music, flirting with girls, drinking free booze. Not a bad life. That would have been a tidy, plausible resolution to the Duran Duran story.

Nothing about Duran Duran has ever been tidy or plausible, though. Greater things awaited. Somehow, this particular mishmash of personalities—Simon's confidence, John's artistry, Nick's clarity of vision, Roger's stability, Andy's musical knowledge—molded the band into something far greater than the sum of their parts. They started to get *good*. Working as a singular unit, each member contributing to the extent of his ability, they honed their signature sound and wrote a bunch of songs that would fly up the charts as this onetime art school punk band evolved into a global pop sensation. By 1980, they were touring the UK as the opening act for new wave artist Hazel O'Connor; by tour's end, they'd fielded offers from two of the UK's leading record companies. They signed with EMI, former home of the Beatles.

Shortly after deciding to form a band, Nick and John set three goals: They'd perform at London's Hammersmith Odeon by 1982, at Wembley Arena by 1983, and at Madison Square Garden by 1984. With the ease of checking off items on a grocery list, Duran Duran hit these goals. They were a glitter-tailed comet, dazzling and unstoppable, no trace of self-doubt or frustration or fear of failure showing on their beautiful painted faces. They were Duran Duran, man. They were going to conquer the world.

CHAPTER TWO: NEW WAVE VOLTRON

ROGER TAYLOR IS a smoldering slab of shirtless man-flesh. This is the opening shot of "Planet Earth," Duran Duran's first music video for the first single released off their 1981 self-titled debut album, the band's first large-scale visual introduction to the world, and everyone is doing his best to make an impression. In Roger's case, this means losing his clothes, good lad. Roger's sculpted shoulders emerge out of wispy clouds; lighting flickers in a glowing sky as he tilts his head back to look at the Earth, which hovers above him. It's not at all clear what's going on; maybe we're witnessing the birth of humanity from the primordial mist, or maybe Roger is a celestial deity. A smoking-hot celestial deity.

"Planet Earth" is directed by Australian video superstar Russell Mulcahy, who built his pre-Duran reputation on visually striking works like the Buggles' "Video Killed the Radio Star" and Ultravox's "Vienna." "Planet Earth" marks the start of a long and fruitful creative collaboration between Mulcahy and Duran Duran. Mulcahy will ultimately direct some of the band's most famous videos—"Rio," "Hungry Like the Wolf," "The Wild Boys," "The Reflex"—and will be behind the helm for the full-tilt lunacy of the band's surreal sci-fi concert film, *Arena (An Absurd Notion)*. Later, he'll find success directing big-budget features, starting with 1986's beloved cult sensation *Highlander*; most recently he was seen coaxing good performances out of various smoldering slabs of shirtless man-flesh on MTV's *Teen Wolf*.

Simon's lyrics for "Planet Earth" are evocative and indecipherable, subject to a billion interpretations. Maybe the song is about floating in the far reaches of space and listening for sounds from a dying earth; there's also a part about rhyming patterns, and a part where Simon sings, "*Bop bop bop, bop bop bop bop bop.*" It's cryptic and unfathomable, but that's new wave for you. New wave doesn't need you to understand it. New wave doesn't want to be coddled. New wave is experimental noise released into an electronic void, chilly and clinical. New wave is punk with the chaotic rage surgically removed, disco exorcised of all traces of soul. New wave is what will play while a fully-operational Skynet obliterates humanity in a fiery blast. New wave is awesome, and so is "Planet Earth."

They're not calling themselves a new wave band, though, not right now. For this moment in time, Duran Duran have embraced New Romanticism, a stylishly cultish and club-based movement which, in 1981, is making a stir in the UK. Epitomized by acts like Spandau Ballet and Visage, the New Romantics dress like world-weary time-travelers from bygone eras in velvet coats and frills; as with new wave, their signature sound is electronic and aloof. Despite some stylistic overlap, New Romanticism isn't exactly where Duran Duran want to be—Duran Duran's dreams involve sold-out amphitheaters, while the New Romantics, arty outsiders at heart, prefer lurking glamorously on the fringes—but right now, the New Romantics are getting noticed, and that makes them useful. The Durans are smart and mercenary, with an instinct for anticipating the zeitgeist; they dress up like fashion-conscious pirates and attach themselves to the New Romantic movement for a hot second, then drift away when the label threatens to become inconvenient.

So Roger is shirtless, and Roger is smoking hot. There's an attempt in this video to nudge Roger closer to the front and center of the band, which is an idea that makes a lot of sense on paper. Roger has James Dean's hair and Brando's eyes and a tendency to look adorably lost and wounded in unguarded moments; the breakout heartthrob potential is strong with this one. Of the five Durans, though, he's the one with the least affinity for the spotlight; he doesn't want to raise a fuss, but given any choice in the matter, he prefers to be left alone in the back of the room with his drum set, thank you very much. As it shakes out, Roger's exhibitionism in "Planet

Earth" will be an anomaly. After this, he'll mostly hover in the background of videos, often looking sheepish and uncomfortable.

Not to be outdone by Roger, Simon also ditches his shirt. He lies demurely on his side, flashing a provocative glimpse of one fuzzy armpit while making bedroom eyes at the camera. Simon is, now and forever, Duran Duran's most foremost star, the one who owns the lion's share of screen time and attention. In this video, he drifts from vignette to vignette: Here, he's embracing a pretty young woman in a fancy hat; there, he's dancing on an inverted crystal pyramid in a chamber of ice. There's no cohesive narrative to found, just a bunch of cool images revolving around a general theme of the four elements: earth, air, fire, water. At one point, random facts scroll across the screen like a computer readout—hey, did you know the oldest known song is the Shaduf Chant?—while the band members pose in the background, looking solemn and lovely.

Leggy knockout John Taylor possesses the daunting bone structure and icy impassivity of a supermodel, both of which he uses to great effect in "Planet Earth." His eyes remain hidden for the duration of the video by a thick sheaf of glossy bangs that fall to his nose, providing a barrier between him and the riffraff. In grand New Romantic style, the wardrobe for the video consists of a metric ton of ruffles in the form of frilly blouses paired with draping scarves and billowy pants tucked into knee boots. Blessed with the ability to look effortlessly stylish in whatever he's wearing, John makes it work.

Some of his bandmates, though, aren't as lucky. Nick's blouse appears to be murdering him. Ruffles erupt from his chest, *Aliens*-style, and slither around his throat, throttling the life out of him. Nick and Andy sport matching thatches of stiff white hair that burst from their heads like dandelions on the cusp of shedding their seeds. Andy's got enough aggressive moxie to pull off his weird hairdo—sure, go ahead and mock his hair, like he gives a rip what you think—but Nick is a disaster. His straw-dry hair is crimped as well as bleached, with weird pinkish patches scattered throughout, like someone started to add some highlights and lost interest halfway through the process. Still in his teens, the baby of the band hasn't sorted out his image yet. Before the year ends, he'll transform himself into a sleek and lovely creature, but right now, he's a work in progress. He's still a cygnet, bits of shell and albumen clinging to his pinfeathers from his recent emergence into the world.

"Planet Earth" is an imperfect video, but as first efforts go, it's an outstanding calling card for the band, establishing them as glamorous beings who go on strange and often supernatural journeys, the likes of which are inaccessible to mortals. Here, they're bopping around the Fortress of Solitude; next year, they'll storm through jungles and battle zombies and cavort with sultry brunettes on the decks of yachts while gliding through azure waters. Someday soon, they'll fight to survive in a post-apocalyptic wasteland. They're not just a band, they're *adventurers*.

Actually, you know what they are? They're *Voltron*. You ever watch *Voltron*? An altered American version of the fabulously-named Japanese animated series *Beast King GoLion*, *Voltron: Defenders of the Universe* first aired on US television in 1984, right at Peak Duran; it centers around five cute intergalactic spaceship pilots who band together to form a gigantic evil-fighting robot. The Duran Duran parallels are, I believe, obvious.

Bear with me here; I'm at least 35% serious. There's something powerful and romantic about a five-person team, a quintet of disparate individuals with different but well-defined strengths and weaknesses who can team up to form something greater than the sum of their parts. This is a dynamic that crops up a whole lot in both anime and live-action *sentai* shows (in the US, *Power Rangers* is the best-known example of the latter) and frequently surfaces in other forms as well. Duran Duran are a five-person team, and, like the *Voltron* pilots (or like the *Gundam Wing* pilots, or like the ladies of *Sailor Moon*... I could go on), the individual band members each bring something unique to the table.

Let's break them down into archetypes: Simon is the leader, the showiest and most charismatic of the group, all personality and swagger, the one most likely to flash you his bare armpit whether you've expressed an interest in seeing it or not. John's the right-hand man, the backup heartthrob, solemn and serious and maybe a little above it all. Andy's the loose cannon, the mouthy one, the comic relief. Roger's the quiet one, the one who outwardly appears to have his act together; his interior might or might not be a seething mess of neuroses. Nick is the weirdo, the savant, the *enfant terrible*. If Duran Duran are a basket of fluffy kittens, Nick is the baby ocelot who somehow got in there by mistake.

Duran Duran set up the five-person team dynamic in the "Planet Earth" video, then promptly shelved it for their second single, "Careless Memories." Compared to the frosty isolation of "Planet Earth," "Careless Memories" is angry and urgent, with a synth line that surges and pulses like a murderer's heartbeat while Simon snarls out bitter lyrics about a bad breakup. For the most part, the band doesn't really *do* songs about romance, failed or otherwise, but "Careless Memories" is a fine exception to that informal rule. It's a scorching, blistering track that nonetheless failed to replicate the chart success of "Planet Earth," maybe because the song is let down by a mopey video involving some anxious piffle about how Simon's girlfriend secretly digs John.

To be fair, the "Careless Memories" video isn't awful. It's just a bit dull, that's all. Directed by Perry Haines and Terry Jones, co-founders of the influential UK fashion magazine *i-D*, the video tells a simple story in straight lines: Simon acts like a prickly ass to his girlfriend, so she begins canoodling with John on the sly, probably because John is staggeringly beautiful and she is not blind. In the video's most exciting moment, Simon gets SO MAD about his crumbling relationship that he snatches a bunch of pink tulips out of a vase and hurls them against a white wall. The five-person team dynamic is nowhere in sight; Andy, Roger, and Nick spend the video lumped together at a table in the corner, like children in exile at a dinner party while the grownups drink too much Blue Nun and hurl tulips around. In 1984, Nick referred to "Careless Memories" as "the worst video we've ever made,"[2] a bold proclamation that was truer then than it is today, now that the band has almost forty years of videos of varying quality under their belts. Contrary to Nick's claim, "Careless Memories" isn't the worst thing they've done. It's disappointing only because Duran Duran are capable of so much more.

Here's an endearing thing about Duran Duran: If there's a perceived misstep in their past, they'll obsess about it, and they'll work furiously to correct it, particularly when it comes to their videos. They're fond of releasing multiple versions, each tweaked and revised to an extent that would make George Lucas mutter something about leaving well enough alone. Sometimes this seems fussy and unnecessary—there are at least six different versions of the "New Moon on Monday" video floating around out there, and let me assure you, the first one got the job done—and sometimes the results are *awesome*. Twenty-four years after the release of "Careless Memories," Duran Duran whipped up a brand-new anime-style video for the song, which played on a gigantic screen behind the band during the 2005 *Astronaut* tour. Directed by visual designer Gary Oldknow, with art by Fumio Obata and Ai Hasegawa, the "Careless Memories" anime features a deliriously gonzo string of events in which animated versions of the band members, dressed like proper *sentai* heroes in bright color-coded suits, fend off multiple waves of attacks from ninjas, killer robots, aliens, and giant fire-breathing lizards. Simon wields his microphone stand like a samurai sword and chops ninjas in two; Roger embeds his cymbals in the skulls of his attackers. Ludicrous geysers of blood spurt in all directions. They're a five-person team, fighting evil and looking fabulous in the process. The Voltron pilots couldn't have done it better.

CHAPTER THREE: THERE WILL BE BOOBS

DURAN DURAN SHOOT the video for "Girls on Film," the third single off of their debut album, in July of 1981. Timing is everything: MTV launches the following month, ushering in the Golden Age of Video. The relationship between Duran Duran and MTV soon becomes symbiotic. Duran Duran, quick to recognize the potential of the music video format, deftly exploit the medium by delivering a series of innovative, buzz-generating, profile-raising videos, while MTV thrives on the attention these rising global superstars bring to the nascent network.

Duran Duran's not bringing this attention to MTV for the "Girls on Film" video, though. In its original form, the "Girls on Film" video can't air—could never air, *still* has never aired—on MTV, for one difficult to ignore reason.

Breasts. It's got a lot of breasts in it.

Mind you, in 1981, bare breasts are not a scandalous sight. Movies released in this decade are teeming with breasts. Actually, that's not quite right; usually they're teeming with boobs. What's the difference, you ask? Mostly, it's a question of cachet. It breaks down loosely along these lines: Meryl Streep flashes a breast in *Silkwood*, whereas those game young actresses in *Hot Dog: The Movie* flash their boobs.

Boobs are omnipresent in eighties pop culture. Watch an R-rated comedy or horror film released during this decade, and odds are pretty good you'll get an eyeful. However, MTV is a basic cable network. Basic cable is subject to the FCC's content regulations for indecency, and thus the boob-filled version of "Girls on Film" is a no-go for MTV.

"Girls on Film" is more than just replete with boobs. It's also—what's the best way to put this?—porny. Yes, that's the word: "Girls on Film" is porny. I don't meant that in a scolding I-know-pornography-when-I-see-it sense; I mean the plot (heh, "plot") of the video is literally based around a variety of porn motifs.

"Girls on Film" is directed by Kevin Godley and Lol Creme, also known as the rock duo Godley & Creme. Their song "Cry" will become a Top 40 hit in 1985, thanks in part to a splashy appearance on an outstanding *Miami Vice* episode, the one where Crockett gets involved with the wrong woman while her husband, a shirtless dirtball played by Ted Nugent, runs around robbing and murdering drug lords and burying their corpses inside their fancy cars in a sand quarry. If you haven't seen it, it's excellent, trust me. Anyway, the lilting strains of "Cry" swell over the final scene as Crockett's lover is being led off in handcuffs while Crockett looks wistful yet exhausted, like he's getting a little fed up with all of his love interests turning out to be felonious scumbags.

Simon's lyrics to "Girls on Film" are world-weary and cynical, telling a story in oblique terms about porn stars, in particular a girl with cherry lipstick smiling for the camera while drowning in blue waters. There's a bite to it, maybe a hint of judgment; at the very least, the girl at the heart of the lyrics seems to be reconsidering her life choices. The video, though? No judgment here. If the video has a theme, this is it: HOORAY FOR BOOBS.

It opens with a credit sequence, of all the damn things, while carpenters build a platform stage and a long runway leading up to it. Duran Duran set up beside the stage and launch into the song while six cheerfully sleazy vignettes take place on the platform in rapid succession:

Vignette #1: Two young women in flimsy negligees saunter down the runway and pose hand-in-hand on the stage next to a red-and-white striped barber's pole, which rests horizontally across two sawhorses. Oh, and the pole is slathered with shaving cream. The women clutch pillows and straddle the pole from either end, then slither their crotches through the cream until they meet at the center, whereupon they engage in a vigorous pillow fight. Their negligees do not survive the battle. At the culmination of the fight—it's impossible to tell who won, and really, it can't possibly matter—the women dismount and kiss.

(Digression: In 2011, Duran Duran—and this is one of those instance where, when I write "Duran Duran," you should feel free to just read that as "Nick Rhodes"—got *super* into Second Life and created an all-Duran zone known as the Duran Duran Universe, complete with underwater dance clubs, luxurious spas, and sundry Duran-themed oddities, like the Simon-dunking wind-mill from the "Wild Boys" video. My curiosity piqued, I slapped together an avatar and entered their realm. Anyway, the *very first place* I visited was a seedy dive containing a room with a striped pole ripe for mounting and a basket of pillows resting beside it, just in case any intrepid souls felt like engaging in a "Girls on Film"-inspired duel. Lingerie optional, I presume. Because I lack an adventurous spirit, I did not mount the pole. I backed slowly out of the room and never again visited the Duran Duran Universe.)

Vignette #2: A gigantic sumo wrestler faces off in the ring against a petite woman clad in a mawashi—the diaperlike sumo undergarment—and a transparent top. After a few moves, she flips him onto his back.

Vignette #3: A sexy nurse in white fishnets and backless heels gives a man a massage. Lots and lots of body oil gets spurted over bare flesh. By the end of the massage, the man lies dead from mysterious causes while the woman saunters off in triumph.

Vignette #4: Holy moly, this is not good. A blonde woman dressed as a kinky cowgirl takes a ride on her bucking steed, who happens to be a muscular young black man wearing a G-string and a horse mask. At the conclusion of her pony ride, she sponges him down while he writhes around in a not especially equine manner.

Well. This is unfortunate.

Bright side first: This is the only moment in the video where the male form is objectified in any way—the sumo wrestler and the man receiving the massage are unclothed but deliberately unsexy—which, what with all the female objectification going on, adds a needed dollop of balance. Still, perhaps *literally comparing a black man to a horse* wasn't the best way to go.

Moving on.

Vignette #5: A woman in a one-piece bathing suit cut up past her hipbones splashes in a kiddie pool and pretends to drown. When a lifeguard arrives to give her mouth-to-mouth resuscitation, she murders him and leaves his lifeless corpse behind in the pool. Maybe she poisons him with her lipstick, maybe she sucks the life right out of him. Duran Duran video vixens are not to be trifled with, y'all. All the women in this video are combatants or murderers, and apart from that blonde lady using that nice young man as a pony, none of them have any practical use for men.

Vignette #6: Two topless women wrestle in mud. They get dirty. So very dirty.

Backstage, naked women splash champagne on their breasts and rub ice cubes on their nipples. Look, it probably gets *very hot* backstage. Improper ventilation can kill.

While all these overheated shenanigans occur, the band members take a passive role, always around but keeping their distance, neither participants nor voyeurs. For most of the video, they perform on the floor next to the stage, relegated to the sidelines; the camera pays them about as much attention as the patrons of a strip club pay the house band. They also appear briefly in the opening moments while the models, clad in hair curlers and bathrobes, get ready backstage. Like the models, the Durans fuss with their hair and apply their makeup and squint at their beautiful reflections in the mirror. They're primping, in other words, their behavior indistinguishable from that of the models, apart from the naked mudwrestling.* They barely interact with the models; Simon bends down to kiss one on the cheek, a chaste pre-show greeting between professionals.

*If "Girls on Film" had featured *Duran Duran* wrestling in the mud while naked, this video would not just be notorious, it'd be legendary. Missed opportunity, lads.

Duran Duran's impassive reaction to all the tawdriness surrounding them is a bracing elixir in the midst of all the cheerily tacky mayhem, the sole element that saves the video from being nothing more than a gratuitous wankfest.** Pornography is sex as a performance, and Duran Duran, like the models, are performers. They're too cool to break a sweat, too sophisticated to openly ogle naked women. They may like breasts and they may like beautiful women—they also like looking beautiful themselves, for what that's worth—but they're here to do a job. There's nothing here they haven't seen before.

**Just so we're clear, there's nothing wrong with gratuitous wankfests. It's just nice to have something a little more substantial, that's all.

So it's the summer of 1981, and Duran Duran have a brand-new, boob-filled, porny music video, and MTV, the world's first network specifically designed to air music videos, is unable to show it. On the surface, this seems like a bad decision on the part of the band, but making a porny video isn't a misstep. It's a calculated business strategy, designed to attract attention—a lot of attention—to Duran Duran.

Boobs are common in the eighties, sure, but pornography is not. This is the pre-internet era, and it's still a few years before the home-video boom reaches a peak, and hence it can be a little tricky to view porn. Thus, porn is a sought-after commodity. "Girls on Film" is a hit song with a video everyone knows about and wants to see, yet few *can* see. Duran Duran have created a demand. They've generated buzz, clever boys.

A shorter, sanitized, boob-free version of "Girls on Film" airs on MTV, while the uncensored video (the *good* version, my breast-loving friends solemnly insist) is shown in nightclubs and other places with relaxed policies regarding the display of exposed mammaries. The buzz continues to grow. The song performs respectably on the charts, reaching the top ten in the UK. The song's a hit; the video is a sensation. Still, the uncensored version won't reach a mass audience until it's released on home video in 1983, whereupon it promptly becomes popular viewing material in the homes of flabbergasted Betamax-owning parents of young girls. Because for all their sophistication, for all their vices, for all their brazen onscreen antics, Duran Duran are beloved by preteens, who adore them and everything they stand for. Boobs and all.

CHAPTER FOUR: ELEPHANTIASIS

DURAN DURAN ARE a polarizing band—for every die-hard Duranie, there's some dudebro at a bar with a pressing need to weigh in on their perceived sucki-tude—but "Hungry Like the Wolf" is not a polarizing song. "Hungry Like the Wolf" is beloved, and rightly so. You've sung rousing renditions at karaoke night, drunk-en strangers joining in to croon their liberal interpreta-tions of the lyrics. You've resisted the urge to do a few impromptu dance moves in the drugstore aisle when it's come on over the sound system. In times of exhaustion and frustration, "Hungry Like the Wolf" has given you life.

The song kicks off with a burst of female laughter, supplied by one of Nick's close friends, Elayne Griffiths, who, two years after the song's 1982 release, will don a tuxedo and serve as the best man at his wedding. From there on out, it's nothing but four minutes of uncomplicated, unbridled joy, as bubbly and irresistible as a bathtub filled with champagne. Close your eyes and listen, and you're somewhere else, somewhere simpler and better. Maybe you're back in the eighties, maybe at a school dance, awkward in your satin dress, the one with the poofy sleeves and the enormous bow at the back, reeking of Love's Baby Soft and strawberry-flavored Maybelline Kissing Potion and brimming with optimism at the promise the night brings. Maybe you're driving around town with your bad-influence friends in the wee hours of the morning, no destination and no cares, the street lights at deserted intersections continuously flashing red to remind you you're out too late. The radio's playing too loud, and you're giddy with adrenaline and the certain knowledge your parents would highly disapprove of this kind of behavior.

Or maybe you're sprinting through the jungle, muscles burning, skin sticky with sweat, shielded from the blazing sun by the lush tropical foliage that rises up to meet the sky. You're no longer sure whether you're predator or prey, but you've never felt more alive.

You know what I'm talking about. You know the video. You grew up in the eighties, and "Hungry Like the Wolf" is coded in your DNA.

"Hungry Like the Wolf" is the second single off of the band's second album, the critical and commercial hit *Rio*. The Russell Mulcahy-directed video, which played in heavy rotation on MTV, established a simple, catchy formula that other musical acts would follow through the eighties and beyond: exquisitely-shot footage of beautiful stars doing weird things in exotic locations.

Duran Duran filmed the video in Sri Lanka during a brief break between recording *Rio* and touring in Australia. It's a showcase for Simon Le Bon, intrepid explorer, who dons a fedora and khakis and does his very best Indiana Jones impression (*Raiders of the Lost Ark* was released the preceding year). As always, Simon carries most of the weight of the video on his broad shoulders. He's fun to watch, brimming with energy, his elastic face and theatrical gestures always falling on just the right side of hammy. The role of music video superstar suits him.

It's a straightforward plot: After making meaningful eye contact with a beautiful dark-skinned woman, played by model Sheila Ming, across a room at a party, Simon pursues her through bustling streets and crowded marketplaces before heading into the jungle, whereupon they unleash their animalistic sides and engage in what is undoubtedly mind-blowingly awesome sex. In Ming's case, the unleashing is literal: A cheetah's face is juxtaposed over her own lovely visage, and, at the moment of their inevitable collision, she lashes out with her claws and rakes Simon across the jaw, leaving angry red gouges on his skin.

(Yes. Absolutely. Between this and the poor oiled-down dude in the horse mask in "Girls on Film," Duran Duran should definitely cool it with videos that explicitly compare black people to animals.)

While Simon goes all Heart of Darkness in his search for his dream woman (in one shot, we see his head rise slowly out of a lagoon, a jaunty hat-tip to *Apocalypse Now*), his bandmates tear around Sri Lanka, on foot and in a jeep, alarming the locals and harassing poor shirt-less urchins in their quest to find their friend. John and Roger are featured heavily here; Nick and Andy only make fleeting appearances, as they both arrived in Sri Lanka a few days after the others, having remained behind in London to finish mixing the *Rio* album.

There's a story Nick tells in interviews, frequently but with a great deal of charm, about landing in Sri Lanka in the sweltering heat, fatigued and dazed from long hours in the studio followed by an interminable overseas flight, stuck wearing head-to-toe leather during the six-hour drive in a rickety truck to the video's location. Upon reaching his destination, heat-sick and dehydrat-ed, he witnessed an elephant lumbering across his path, whereupon he assumed he was hallucinating. It's an anecdote that encapsulates the essence of Duran Duran: glamorous, impractical, ludicrous, surreal.

Like many of the videos Mulcahy made with the band, the structure of "Hungry Like the Wolf" is both nonline-ar and deliberately inconsistent. Think of the video as a jigsaw puzzle bought at a yard sale and completed by a drunkard on an all-night bender: Some pieces are missing, and some pieces are jammed into the wrong places, and some pieces seem to come from an entirely different puzzle. At the heart of the video, there's a simple, coherent story: Simon falls for a beautiful woman and goes on a quest to find her. Watch it again, though, and you'll see the trick: It moves forward and backward in time, but even if you untangle the chronology, it still doesn't *quite* makes sense, and that's the beauty. You'd grow tired of viewing the same short film over and over again, no matter how well crafted it might be, but you can watch "Hungry Like the Wolf" again, and again, and again.

During the same Sri Lankan sojourn, Mulcahy and the band shot two other videos. A smaller, slower, quieter song than "Hungry Like the Wolf," "Save a Prayer" has a video to match, serene and contemplative, worlds away from the boisterous chaos of its predecessor. The "Save a Prayer" video is unhampered by plot, even one as uncomplicated as "Simon tears Sri Lanka apart in his search for a smoking-hot woman"; it consists only of peaceful, meditative footage of the band members in rural areas of the country: strolling barefoot on beaches under darkening lavender skies, strumming guitars while lounging on the sand, wandering through stone temples in the shadows of gigantic Buddha sculptures, hanging out in the tree branches above a lagoon populated with elephants. During filming of the latter scene, Andy toppled off his branch, accidentally ingested some elephant-befouled water, and became badly ill, leading to canceled tour dates and a lengthy recuperation. Rough on poor Andy, of course, but ultimately worth it; it's a great shot. "Save a Prayer" also contains a delightful sequence in which John (shirtless) and Nick (pantless) cling to each other while riding on the back of an elephant, which sprays them with water from its trunk while they erupt in delighted laughter; it is both the most outrageously charming moment in any Duran Duran video, past or present, and the most blatantly homoerotic moment in any Duran Duran video made prior to 1984, which is when "The Wild Boys" will set a daring new bar for Duran-based homoerotica.

"Save a Prayer" is lovely, tranquil, and *maaaaaybe* just a little bit boring. It's a good video; it's a great travelogue for Sri Lanka, land of untouched beaches, shimmering temples, and fetching British pop stars scampering around without any pants on. It's worlds better than "Lonely in Your Nightmare," the last and least of the band's three Sri Lankan videos, which features a young woman, played by model Vanya Seager (who also briefly appears in "Save a Prayer"), tossing and turning glamorously in bed while dreaming about Simon. It's beautifully shot—aficionados of Maxfield Parrish's ethereal, airborne paintings will note Mulcahy's stylistic tributes to his compositions—but stagnant.

Doesn't matter. The video is filler, an afterthought, a slapped-together side dish of spinach salad at Christmas dinner, overshadowed by the rich, meaty main course of

"Hungry Like the Wolf." (Continuing on with this belabored metaphor, "Save a Prayer" is a light dessert, maybe a fruit sorbet to cleanse the palate and ease digestion after eating an array of rich foods.)

"Hungry Like the Wolf" is immortal and ubiquitous. It's become a form of shorthand for talking about the eighties: Invoke "Hungry Like the Wolf," and you've instantly transported your audience to a very specific moment in time. Filmmakers know this well—after all, the song has popped up on the soundtracks of over fifty movies and TV episodes. Yoplait briefly featured it in a commercial in 2014 until Duran Duran put a stop to that nonsense, because unless someone comes out with, say, a champagne-infused yogurt flecked with gold leaf and studded with snowberries gathered under a blue moon on a starless night, Duran Duran are not the kind of guys to shill for yogurt. Duran Duran are the kind of guys to ride elephants and stroll barefoot on white beaches and get into erotically-charged tussles with beautiful women in far-off locales. Duran Duran are the kind of guys to give the world the treasure of "Hungry Like the Wolf," and for that we are all grateful.

CHAPTER FIVE: WASTRELS ON A YACHT

THE FIRST DURAN to appear in the opening moments of the 1982 "Rio" video is Nick, seen lying on his stomach on a dock in a tropical island paradise, binoculars raised to his eyes, zooming in on the tanned, toned ass of a swimsuit-clad sunbather lolling nearby. It's a rare display of unadorned, unapologetic lechery from Nick, and it throws down the gauntlet: Those with a limited tolerance for hijinks and tomfoolery best look elsewhere for their entertainment fix.

Not many looked elsewhere. "Rio" is adored by some and mocked by others, but, as with "Hungry Like the Wolf," *everybody's* seen it. The "Rio" video is a joyously silly pop art celebration, saturated with the dazzling hues of the eighties: aqua, orchid, azure, fuchsia. Shot by Russell Mulcahy while the band members were on a working vacation in Antigua, "Rio" is a celebration of what it means to be Duran Duran in 1982: young, rich, beautiful, foolish, and teeming with more joie de vivre than a single band should be expected to contain.

All five Durans spend the video in pursuit of the sun-bather, the Rio of Simon's lyrics, who rises from the waves and strides onto the beach in a low-cut swimsuit with a sheathed knife strapped to her thigh à la Ursula Andress in *Doctor No*, then kicks Roger in the stomach and knocks him on his ass for having the temerity to approach her. As sophisticated and urbane as the Durans all are, Rio is too much for them to handle. Throughout the video, as the boys jockey for her attention, she'll alternately spurn them, mock them, ignore them, stalk them, attack them, and try to drown them in the waves.

Rio is played by model Reema Ruspoli, known simply as Reema, who, in a move that's staggeringly on the nose for a charter member of music video royalty, will go on to marry an Italian prince. Reema is a ringer for the *other* Rio, the dark-haired beauty painted by Patrick Nagel for the famous *Rio* album cover. Nagel, who died unexpectedly in 1984 at the peak of his popularity, was the quintessential artist for this moment in time; bedroom walls in the eighties were covered with prints of his instantly recognizable works, his stylized line drawings of sultry dark-haired women in various states of undress (Nagel first found fame as an illustrator for *Playboy*) brought to life with pops of color. At this stage in their stylistic evolution, Duran Duran embody Nagel's sleek aesthetic. In the "Rio" video, they languidly drape themselves around the deck of a yacht while wearing impeccably tailored silk suits, designed by chic

London couturier Antony Price, in colors that could be swiped straight from Nagel's palette: cream, aqua, sky blue, crimson (Andy, always the outlier, is clad in black).

In "Rio," the boys ooze sophistication from their pores, even when they're doing goofy crap like tossing each other overboard or getting tangled in fishing nets or pretending to play saxophones. I'm roughly twice as old now as John Taylor was when Duran Duran filmed this video, and I'm keenly aware I possess less than half his innate style and savoir faire. John possesses the gift of looking preternaturally elegant and unruffled, like he was born to drink champagne on yachts (whereas Simon, apparently, was born to crew them: Filming "Rio" sparked a lifelong love of boating in him, one that continued even after a near-fatal experience in 1985 when a yacht he co-owned capsized during the Fastnet Race, trapping him inside and sparking feverish global headlines about his narrow escape from death. Simon never does anything on a modest scale).

In his memoir, John writes that critics in Great Britain viewed the "Rio" video as "an arrogant portrayal of the worst traits of Thatcherite self-interest."[3] Sure. "Rio" is fabulous, but the Brits have a point. "Rio," released during a time of ever-mounting economic inequality and anxiety throughout the UK, fetishizes symbols of wealth: the yacht, the champagne that splashes from the sky onto Rio's abdomen, the galloping horse Simon inexplicably rides down the beach. The pleasures found in "Rio" are reserved for the ultra-rich, the elite, the Durans of the world. The use of yachts in music videos to signify mad riches has since become hackneyed—the comedy trio The Lonely Island rustled up a Grammy nomination in 2009 for "I'm on a Boat," their gleeful satire of this über-specific video subgenre—but Duran Duran claimed this territory first in a big, showy manner.

The flip side to all this gloss and decadence is "(Waiting for the) Night Boat," which the band, ever fans of multitasking, filmed simultaneously with "Rio" in Antigua. Where "Rio" is carefree and luxurious, "Night Boat" is ratty, ragged, and menacing. "Night Boat" is also, just FYI, one of the greatest things Duran Duran have ever done.

What, you've never seen "Night Boat"? Don't feel bad about that; I didn't know this video existed until 2011, almost thirty years after it was made. The song, from the band's first album, was never released as a single; the video didn't receive significant airplay on MTV, nor did it make the cut on *Greatest*, a two-disk video collection released on DVD in 2003 (*Greatest* did manage to squeeze in five different versions of the "New Moon on Monday" video, which is the sort of thing that makes me question the band's priorities and, just possibly, their collective sanity).

"Night Boat" opens with the band members loitering around a dock in Antigua. Gone are the silk suits; the boys wear vacation-appropriate street clothes, mostly logo tees and sneakers (Nick, who doesn't really *do* street clothes, wears a long-sleeved black shirt buttoned up to his throat, paired with matching pants and red leather shoes; it's a little fussy and impractical for bumming around a tropical paradise with a group of close friends, but constant maintenance is the price of remaining perpetually fashion-forward). Apart from the five Durans, nobody's in sight; a dangling radio handset, unnoticed by the boys, crackles into life and broadcasts a frantic mayday from a ship at sea.

A murky unease settles over the group. Roger hides in a shed, muttering to himself. A mirror shatters for no reason. Simon, who'd been sitting on the dock looking glamorous and inscrutable, begins spouting a little Shakespeare while Nick looks politely bored but wary, like he's not sure whether Simon's making a bid for attention, or if something about him is genuinely... off.

Night falls. The weirdness accelerates. John shrieks and flees in sudden terror, babbling at an unseen assailant to leave him alone. And then the zombies attack.

Right. Should've mentioned. There are zombies. "Night Boat" is a full-blown zombie film condensed into five perfect minutes of creepy atmosphere and mounting terror. Antigua, it seems, is teeming with zombies. The comparatively gentle Afro-Caribbean voodoo-related zombies, mind you, not the diseased and/or radioactive flesh-eating revenants prevalent in pop culture today;

they hide in trees and slither under the dock and stalk the boys around the island. They converge on John first, surrounding him and tearing his clothes off his body. Substitute crazed fans for the zombies, and you're probably getting a decent glimpse into John's daily life during this particular point in his career.

The Durans fall to the zombies one by one, seduced and corrupted and lured away to a ghostly ship in the harbor. Simon storms around the island in a black trench coat, consorting with a creepy lady zombie while growing increasingly spooky and malevolent. Upon becoming a zombie himself, Nick blossoms forth in a billowy white shirt, hair teased out to its full glory, wearing a full face of heavy, well-applied makeup instead of the lighter, more vacation-appropriate version he sported earlier. Nick is the most Duran of the Durans, the one who most neatly encapsulates all the qualities that make this band so irresistible, the over-the-top glamour and the art and the style and the ridiculous pretensions. If he must be a zombie, well then, he's going to be the most beautiful zombie on the whole damn zombie boat.

By video's end, all will have succumbed, save for pure-hearted Roger, who's left standing alone on the island, forlorn and fatigued, watching as the zombie boat takes to the sea with his fallen friends on board. The zombie boat is probably the "Rio" yacht, come to think of it, because surely even Duran Duran wouldn't rent two different yachts during the same vacation (they might, actually). Using the same boat makes sense: "Rio" and "Night Boat" are opposites that define each other, day and night, light and dark, heaven and hell. "Rio" thrives in sunlight and open spaces; "Night Boat" slithers through the dark cracks. "Night Boat" is the cold, sick wave of exhaustion and regret that comes after "Rio"'s weeklong daiquiri-fueled fiesta. Party on the sun-drenched deck of that yacht as much as you want, all you beautiful young Durans, but the night boat comes for everybody in the end.

CHAPTER SIX: DURANIMOSITY

GUYS HATE DURAN Duran. You may have noticed.

Yes, of course, I know, #notallguys. Some of the most ardent and informed Duranies have a Y chromosome; similarly, a great many dilettante fans, the ones who wouldn't label themselves Duranies but who've been known to hum along to "Hungry Like the Wolf" if it happens to be playing, are male. Go to a Duran Duran concert, and the audience will be more or less an even mix of men and women. I've opened this essay with a sweeping and unfair generalization, but I bet if you average it out, my statement stands: Guys hate Duran Duran.

More accurately, they *despise* the band, often with a wild-eyed zeal, the kind associated with lunatics on the N train howling about the looming apocalypse. Hatred of Duran Duran is a deeply personal thing.

If you're female and a Duranie, I'm not telling you anything you don't know. You've mentally braced yourself while talking to a bunch of guys and the topic drifts to music. When asked to name your favorite band, you've faced the resulting blast of withering scorn and condescension too many times to count. Being a cowardly sort, I've spent a lifetime learning how to mitigate that scorn, how to punctuate my responses with self-deprecating laughter, how to deflect insults and dodge the subject.

No more, I say. I'm done with self-deprecation and deflection. Fuck that noise. Duran Duran is my favorite band, full stop. What are you going to do about it?

From the results of my unscientific surveys on this topic, the opinions of members of the anti-Duran contingent usually fall into one of these two camps:

1) Their music is terrible, or:

2) They're a boy band, and boy bands are terrible.

I'll allow the first point on an agree-to-disagree basis, because terribleness of music is a subjective thing, but the "boy band" point collapses under scrutiny. Even when the term isn't used pejoratively (and let's be real, isn't "boy band" always meant in at least a somewhat pejorative manner?), it doesn't apply to Duran Duran, unless you're using it to mean a band in which every member is in possession of a penis, in which case... welcome to the boy band club, Rolling Stones! You too, KISS. Red Hot Chili Peppers, Aerosmith, nice to see you as well, though it's getting awfully crowded in here. In any case, Duran Duran check off none of the requisite boy-band boxes: They aren't a prefabricated group (i.e.

the members weren't assembled inorganically by a Svengali-esque manager or producer), they've always maintained singular control over their own image, they write all their own songs, they play all their own instruments, they don't sing in multipart harmony with each other, they don't dance (if the "New Moon on Monday" video shows us nothing else, it's that they do not and should not dance), and they have no earthly use for syrupy love ballads.

Let's zoom back to 1983, which is right about when the male animosity toward the band—forgive me, but I'm going to get *really cute* and refer to it as "Duranimosity"—starts to pick up steam, as Duran Duran navigate the transition from "popular and successful group" to "worldwide phenomenon." In between albums—they've already experienced the celebrated success of *Rio* and have yet to record *Seven and the Ragged Tiger*—they score their first number-one hit in the UK (number four in the US) with "Is There Something I Should Know?" They're at the top of the pile, and the video shows it. Directed by Russell Mulcahy, their preferred co-conspirator, the video is cool and artsy, with deliberate stylistic nods to Escher drawings and Magritte paintings. The band members are dressed identically in blue button-down shirts with matching white ties; it's a clear visual nod to the Beatles, to whom the band were increasingly compared during this time.

Uh oh.

Speed ahead to February of 1984: Duran Duran appear on the cover of *Rolling Stone* with a headline christening them THE FAB FIVE, in what can only be seen as a deeply opportunistic attempt to court those aforementioned Beatles comparisons.

Before you start to fume, I'm going to stop you right here and point out the obvious: No one should be making any such comparisons. Duran Duran may be awesome, but the Beatles are the Beatles. If you pit Duran Duran in a head-to-head matchup against the Beatles, they get massacred in almost all categories: ability, innovation, level of fame, depth of catalogue, and influence over other artists. It's not entirely certain Duran Duran would defeat the Beatles in a no-holds-barred bare-knuckles cage match, though as a personal aside, that's something I would give my hypothetical firstborn to watch. However, in terms of the ability to whip fans into a frenzy, and particularly the ability to imprint every band member as a separate and distinct individual upon the public consciousness, the comparisons start seeming a smidgen less blasphemous.

I'm going to pick a Duran-contemporaneous example to show you what I mean: By standard metrics, U2 are more critically and commercially successful than Duran Duran. Right? I'm not trying to knock Duran Duran by stating this; I'm just pointing to the stats: U2 have had more hit singles (31 hits on the *Billboard* Hot 100 to Duran Duran's 21), more awards (22 Grammys to Duran Duran's two), and more record sales (Duran Duran have sold over a hundred million records; U2 have sold a reported 170 million). If we're going to haphazardly toss around Beatles comparisons, maybe it makes more sense to toss them in the general direction of U2.

And yet... okay, sure, everybody can readily identify Bono, by both name and appearance. He's an undisputed star, globally famous for his music, his social and political activism, and his philanthropy. Most people probably know The Edge as well. And then after that... well, there's a guy named Adam on bass and a guy named Larry on drums; if I close my eyes, I *think* I can picture them, but I might be confusing Larry with, I dunno, Stewart Copeland or someone. Granted, I'm a mere dabbler in the wide world of U2, but even still, throughout U2's forty-year history, there's been no concerted attempt outside of the music press to brand the band members, Bono excepted, as distinct individuals instead of a singular entity.

Not so for Duran Duran. Because of their videos, because of their symbiotic relationship with MTV, because of the teen magazines, because of the high level of public interest in their personal lives, Duran Duran's overall level of recognition for all five band members is higher than U2's. Even the people who are convinced John, Andy, and Roger are brothers, or maybe triplets (we have all met those people), well, at least they know the band has three members with a last name of Taylor. Simon, John, Nick, Andy, and Roger don't have anywhere near the same level of widespread visual recognition as John, Paul, George, and Ringo... but they come a whole lot closer than most groups.

So if you were looking for reasons to hate Duran Duran, maybe you could point to the video for "Is There Something I Should Know?", or to that *Rolling Stone* cover. They think they're the Beatles! That's pretty obnoxious, right? After all, Liam Gallagher inspired some well-earned mockery when he proclaimed in the *Sunday Times* in 1996 that Oasis is "...better than the Beatles," then went on to say, in a vastly entertaining rant, "I reckon we've pissed all over the Beatles ... They're not the best band in the world—we are!"[4] Liam spent most of the nineties running his mouth off in hilarious diatribes like this—it's what he's known for, really—and yet guys don't hate Oasis. Not in droves, not in the same all-encompassing way they hate Duran Duran.

Here's my theory about what lies at the core of all this Duranimosity: Women like Duran Duran, and things women like often tend to be anathema to men. For whatever reason or combination of reasons, Duran Duran appeal to women. Some of it is their appearance: They're a bunch of hot guys, and—brace yourselves, I've got another sweeping generalization coming up—women are often partial to hot guys. Funny how that works. Factor in the band's long-running obsessions with the worlds of art and fashion—both often viewed, through a narrow lens, as "unmanly" pursuits—and all of a sudden the rampant Duranimosity starts looking like a defensive reaction. In short, Duran Duran are covered in girl-cooties, and some dudes are terribly worried it might be contagious.

It's not news, this idea that men and boys reflexively scorn and devalue things women and girls find important. Evidence for this isn't merely anecdotal: A well-publicized 2016 report at the statistics-centric website FiveThirtyEight.com showed that male users of the website IMDB.com tend to give aggressively low scores to movies and TV shows geared toward women.[5] FiveThirtyEight describes this behavior as "sabotage"; I'd agree with that.

(In case you're wondering, per the FiveThirtyEight report, the reverse doesn't hold true: Male IMDB users will give low scores to women-oriented shows like *Sex and the City* to drive the overall rating down, whereas female users don't demonstrate the same behavior by giving low marks to, say, the *Transformers* oeuvre.)

In the face of rampant Duranimosity, the goal, I think, should be to deal with it the way the band members do. The Durans are impervious to scorn and mockery; criticism bounces off their beautiful gold-plated hides. All of them, even mild-mannered Roger, have the robust egos required to face mounds of abuse, day in and day out. When Duran Duran were announced as the headlining act of the pre-opening ceremony concert in Hyde Park for the 2012 London Olympics, some corners of the UK press scorned the pick, deriding them as irrelevant; when asked for a response, Simon just laughed. "We're Duran Duran," he told BBC Radio Five. "We've been taking crap from all different angles for many, many years ... There's no way that anybody can make us go away by saying nasty things about us."[6]

Well said, Simon. If criticism had the ability to affect Duran Duran, they'd be shells of their former selves by now, nothing more than crushed, crumpled, withered husks of Durans. They are not. They are hale and hearty, their sturdy egos unbroken, their senses of self-worth intact. They're *Duran Duran*, damn it. Long may they serve as an example for us all.

CHAPTER SEVEN: NICK RHODES IS PRETTIER THAN YOU

NICK RHODES IS prettier than you. Please don't take that personally; it's 1984, and Nick is prettier than everyone. He's prettier than Madonna humping the stage in a wedding gown while performing "Like a Virgin" at the MTV Video Music Awards. He's prettier than Brooke Shields posing on Michael Jackson's arm at the Grammys. He might even be prettier than Sade in the "Smooth Operator" video, though that's too close to call. Nick is gorgeous, a careful study in the art of loveliness, eyes dramatically lined and shaded, cheeks contoured, lips painted, every strand of hair teased and styled. He's worn makeup consistently since the late seventies, and by now he's become *really good* at applying it; if this whole pop-legend-in-the-making thing weren't going so well for him, he could pick up a nice chunk of change freelancing backstage at runway shows during Fashion Week.

Nick is tiny—not all that short, but petite, like he subsists on a diet of starlight and moonbeams and maybe the occasional dainty sip of Armand de Brignac, served in a calla lily. He looks like a magical creature, some form of elf or pixie. The color of his hair seems to change with the phases of the moon, a fresh hue every time he steps out in public: white, then brown, then red, then gold. It always looks fabulous.

The only people who can give him a run for his money in the beauty department are his bandmates. Look at them performing onstage during the 1984 Sing Blue Silver tour in the video for "The Reflex," which is shot by—you guessed it—Russell Mulcahy. Everybody looks fantastic, nothing but clear glowing skin and great smiles and shiny hair. They look better than pop stars should, really. They're so, so pretty, even Andy. Andy is known as the plain one of the group, comparatively speaking, and yet there's nothing wrong with Andy's bone structure. Andy's a dish.

Nick is beautiful, and everyone has noticed. Joe Elliott, lead singer of Def Leppard, once mused of Duran Duran, "As much as they were all heterosexuals, you could understand why gay men would fancy them. Especially Nick Rhodes. I mean, even we fancied Nick Rhodes."[7] With his lined eyes and his lipstick, Nick is playing hardball with androgyny, messing around with the notion of having either a predominately masculine or predominately feminine appearance. Designer Antony Price, the man responsible for those snazzy silk suits in the "Rio" video, has said of his longtime friend's penchant for makeup, "He's never done it to look like a woman but to be a better-looking man."[8] Nick is a great-looking man who simultaneously looks like a great-looking woman.

Nick is a straight man—all five Durans have consistently identified as straight and cisgender—who is comfortable enough in his own skin to experiment with gender boundaries on a huge public stage. What he's doing isn't drag—it's pretty far from it, actually—but he's challenging the idea of how men are supposed ("supposed") to look, by incorporating elements of how women are supposed (again, "supposed") to look.

Nick has, to my knowledge, appeared in full drag in public only once*, in the 1997 video for "Out of My Mind," in which he dresses up as an eighteenth-century courtesan in a corset, voluminous skirts, and a tall powdered wig and flounces around a decaying castle in the Czech Republic. He looks, of course, fantastic. At one point in the video, he also wears a green satin suit and makes out with an evil bald lady with tattoos all over her scalp while his head melts away like a big wax candle, so the sight of him in a fancy gown, while dazzling, is maybe not the most memorable part of the video. "Out of My Mind" is a strange, strange beast.

*Okay, there's also that segment on a 1993 episode of MTV's *House of Style* in which Simon, Nick, and host Cindy Crawford go on a mad shopping spree at Sears, whereupon Nick and Simon model sensible poly-blend housedresses and lacy frocks for Cindy. Nick wears clothes well; he looks good in dresses. As does Simon.

Granted, Duran Duran are insulated from the public by their money and fame (Nick is also partially inoculated against rumors about his sexuality by his 1984 marriage to model-slash-department store heiress Julie Anne Friedman), but even still, you have to admire the guts required by Nick, the dainty kid with the pretty face, to go out into the world in full makeup, day after day. In the queer-hostile environment of the eighties, there's a boldness to Duran Duran's willingness to aggressively bring a cultivated style of feminized male beauty into the mainstream.

Not that Duran Duran are alone in this—Boy George, for one, is doing much the same thing—and not that Nick, at this time in his young life, is a paragon of enlightened attitudes when it comes to moving outside of established gender roles. Here's a fun quote from Nick, as recounted in Neil Gaiman's *Duran Duran: The First Four Years of the Fab Five***: "The thought of something like a woman fireman is very silly. I believe women should be paid the same for doing the same jobs as men, but there again, I'd still much rather women be feminine." [9] I'm going to go ahead and generously assume this bit of mind-blowing cognitive dissonance is less Nick's carefully-considered worldview and more the kind of off-the-cuff nitwittery that sometimes results when interviewers stick microphones in the faces of very young pop stars.

**Yep. That Neil Gaiman. In 1984, Neil Gaiman wrote a book about Duran Duran. It's pretty good!

Here in 2017, pop music needs more Duran Durans, more Boy Georges, more Grace Joneses, more Annie Lennoxes, more Pete Burnses, more performers willing to play around with conventional gender norms, because even as fluid sexuality gains more mainstream acceptance, it sometimes seems like the male-female divide is widening, and Janelle Monáe, as much of a force of nature as she is, can't be expected to bridge it all on her own. With key exceptions—Janelle, Miley, Halsey, P!nk—today's female pop stars have long hair and wear pretty dresses; their male counterparts keep their locks short and shun makeup. It's fine, but it's *boring.* Right now, androgyny's best hope may lie with Ruby Rose, the openly queer DJ-slash-model-slash-*Orange Is the New Black* star, known for her ability to spark serious crushes in women who otherwise identify as heterosexual. Rose wears her hair cropped short and punkish, and she's got tattoos for days; there's usually a snarl on her red, red lips. She's small and petite, with dainty features, a pointed jaw, and beautiful eyes, which she accentuates with a great deal of well-applied smoky makeup. Whether you prefer men or women or both or neither, it's hard to deny she's gorgeous. Matter of fact, she looks a lot like Nick Rhodes.

CHAPTER EIGHT: "TERRIBLE. HORRIBLE. VILE!"

THIS ESSAY'S TITLE comes courtesy of the ever-fabulous Nick Rhodes, who, in the documentary *Sing Blue Silver*, snarls those words backstage after a performance, bristling with indignation, hair and makeup flawless, arms crossed, cigarette clutched between two slim fingers. He's airing his grievances with the inadequate stage lighting, which left him fumbling in darkness for much of the show; his bandmates, who are all obviously familiar with this line of argument from Nick, nod at appropriate intervals in between swigs of beer.

Later on, Nick will sit down with a pair of lighting directors to hash out a solution. An intricate conversational waltz ensues. They're treading carefully around their tiny, powerful employer, though they're visibly frustrated at the prospect of changing things around this late in the game; Nick is faultlessly polite and sympathetic to their woes, but unyielding. One of the lighting guys delicately suggests the problem might be all in Nick's decorative head—"You're bright up there, I thought, so it is a psychological thing, too"—whereupon

Nick calmly shuts down this line of thought with an ironclad rejoinder: "But I couldn't actually *see*."

We never find out the resolution to this conflict—right at that moment, Roger Taylor wanders directly in front of the documentary camera with his pants sexily unbuttoned, which is enough to yank attention away from the discussion—but it's probably safe to assume Nick gets his way. Nick doesn't lose many battles.

Directed by Michael Collins, with concert footage shot by Russell Mulcahy, *Sing Blue Silver* follows Duran Duran around on the North American leg of their 1984 world tour, right at the apex of the band's global fame. It burbles with the prickly, unstable energy of life on the road, punctuated by an endless series of concerts played before endless crowds of screaming fans, the noise level never less than a roar. If you have predominately warm feelings toward Duran Duran, *Sing Blue Silver* will strengthen your love. If you can't stand Duran, *Sing Blue Silver* will hone your hatred into something white-hot and lethal. *Sing Blue Silver* is pure, uncut, grade-A pharmaceutical Duran Duran. The Durans are shown at their best, and they're shown at their worst, and sometimes it gets difficult to tell which is which. *Sing Blue Silver* reveals the Durans boiled down to their essence, warts and all.

Oh, that's a lie. Duran Duran have no warts. John Taylor had a wart once, maybe, but he glanced at it through lovely but cold eyes, and it withered away in the face of his icy hauteur and regal beauty, never to return.

Sing Blue Silver kicks off with a press conference, in which the Durans set about ruthlessly charming the socks off the American media while celebrating the start of their tour. Spirits are high: An innocent query about the ages of the band members when they learned to play their instruments evolves into a cheeky series of double entendres (punch line: "Roger needs two hands for his!"). It's *A Hard Day's Night*, only with masturbation jokes. The boys are quick on the uptake, brimming with personality and good cheer.

Except for Roger. Roger is being a good sport, because Roger is never anything less than polite and accommodating, but he doesn't want to be here. You can see it in his expression, which hovers somewhere between trapped and agonized; he hates this sort of thing, having to be ribald and witty while making off-the-cuff comments in front of a crowd.

Backstage, Duran Duran gear up for a performance. It's high-octane chaos, because the Durans do everything at maximum volume. They don't so much enter rooms as descend upon them like a barbarian horde. They storm around and whoop and bellow; Andy and Simon suck helium from balloons and collapse into paroxysms of giggle fits at their resulting high-pitched voices. Nick, meanwhile, is utterly transfixed by his stand-up *Galaga* arcade game. Nick, we see, is a dangerous *Galaga* obsessive. The concert is ready to begin, and the band members are being herded like unruly cats toward the stage, but Nick won't budge. He remains at his game, rapt, until one of their handlers wraps his arms around his waist, scoops him up, and, as Nick wails like a feral creature, bodily carries him to the stage.

Agatha Christie's Miss Marple, aged amateur detective, solves mysteries in her quaint English village largely through use of archetypes: By drawing parallels between crime suspects and people she's known throughout her long life, she applies her vast knowledge of human behavior to ferret out the identity of murderers. Faced with Nick Rhodes, Miss Marples would be flummoxed. There is no parallel to Nick; Nick is his own unique entity.

A media blitz ensues, a barrage of press conferences, photo shoots, television shows, interviews. Simon and Nick go on a radio show and field questions from fans. A love-struck caller wants to know if John has any plans to get married. Simon and Nick chuckle good-naturedly, then Nick removes his headset and turns to the host, suddenly icy and deadly. "Get rid of the get-married one," he says quietly.

The Durans travel from city to city, either on their sleek private jet or in limos that sail through cold, snowy streets, followed by a procession of gigantic trailers transporting their set and their gear. On board their jet, they play Parcheesi to kill time, they read, they nap, they drink. They're shepherded around cities on planned excursions, usually surrounded by members of the press. In Washington, they visit the Hoover Building, where star-struck Feds let them fondle their guns; in Atlanta, they're the guests of honor at a corporate shindig held by tour sponsor Coca-Cola. A somewhat woozy John is invited up on stage to address the Coke executives. Clutching his drink, he cheerfully proclaims his preference for Pepsi.

Throughout *Sing Blue Silver*, Andy is—and this is a strange comment to make in regard to Andy—absolutely adorable. He's in his element; touring agrees with him. He's chipper and charming in interviews, he's rambunctious backstage, he's a dynamo while perform-ing. He's having a good time.

Simon, obviously, is the star. The focus always drifts to him, whether he's pulling horrifically ill-timed pranks (feigning a broken arm on the day of their big concert at the Oakland Coliseum, the concert Mulcahy plans to use as the basis for their big-budget concert film, *Arena*) or debating the merits of changing his clothes in full view of the documentary cameras.

The concerts are a swarming mass of humanity. Girls scream and sob and howl for the band, sometimes collapsing on the floor from the overwhelming wave of emotion. Outside a venue, a trio of cute young women cajole a bouncer for backstage passes. They might be groupies, though they don't look the part; they're dressed in 1984's finest preppy chic, baggy sweaters and button-down shirts paired with short feathered hair. They are—forgive me, ladies, I don't mean this unkindly—absolute dingbats. When grilled on their Duran Duran knowledge, they're unable to name a single band member. "You're the worst fans I've ever come across," the bouncer tells them sternly. He is correct; they are terrible. Then he gives them passes anyway, because he's a softie and they're totally cute. "Are we going to be on MTV?" they ask.

Far more endearing are a pair of pre-teen girls, both rocking kicky new wave haircuts and wearing Ray-Bans paired with too-large chauffeur caps, who complain in a world-weary manner that the Durans are *waaaay* too old. They're insufferable, yet sort of wonderful. In four years, they'll probably be backpacking across Europe, caging joints from mohawk-sporting French boys and griping that Depeche Mode have gotten too mainstream.

The band members sit down with Russell Mulcahy to spitball ideas for the shoot for *Arena*. "I've got *loads* of ideas," says Nick, stubble visible beneath his makeup. "Great!" Mulcahy replies, bravely. Nick does indeed have *loads* of ideas. He describes them in intricate detail, complete with expressive hand gestures, while Mulcahy looks vaguely gobsmacked.

Everyone's having fun except Roger. Post-performance, sitting with Andy in the back of a chauffeured car, surrounded on all sides by screaming fans, Roger, a known agoraphobe, begins to come unraveled. He's teary and shaky and seems to be on the verge of a panic attack; probably the only thing holding him together is the awareness of being filmed. Andy gently talks him down from the proverbial ledge, keeping up a relaxed patter while showing off the various cuts and blisters on his hands from playing his guitar and coaxing Roger into comparing battle scars. It's a lovely moment. Andy's time in Duran Duran will end poorly amidst a flurry of lawsuits and acrimony, but right here, he's just a guy with a good heart helping out a friend in distress.

After their final show, Andy, Simon, and John smash themselves together backstage into one prolonged, fervent, sweaty, meaty, teary, shirtless hug. Dead-eyed with something beyond exhaustion, Roger glances at his embracing bandmates, his expression bleak, then slumps over to the catering table to grab a beer. He flops on his back on a sofa and gazes into the void, the thousand-yard stare of the fatigued and despondent. At this moment, Duran Duran is the most famous band in the world, and Roger wants nothing more to do with it.

CHAPTER NINE: DANCING WHILE THE BOMBS FALL

DURAN DURAN IS the band you want to be dancing to when the bombs fall. Simon once made that claim in an interview, and it sounds pretty good to me. If "The Wild Boys" happens to be blasting while I'm obliterated into ashes or melted into a smear of radioactive grease, I won't have any complaints.

About the music, I mean.

To grow up in the eighties was to be surrounded by sweeping Cold War paranoia and wholly valid fears about nuclear proliferation and the acute possibility of imminent annihilation, fears which infused pop music. You could slap together a damn fine mixtape consisting solely of chart-friendly tunes about nuclear Armageddon: Nena's "99 Luftballons," Ultravox's "All Stood Still," Sting's "Russians," John Foxx's "Underpass," Orchestral Manoeuvres in the Dark's "Enola Gay," Men at Work's "It's a Mistake," Kate Bush's "Breathing." In the mid-eighties, Duran Duran produced two videos with strong post-apocalyptic themes: "Union of the Snake," off of 1983's *Seven and the Ragged Tiger* album, and "The Wild Boys," from their 1984 concert album, *Arena*.

"Union of the Snake" is a slinky, sinister little number, shoehorning a ton of enigmatic menace into two short verses, an endlessly repeating refrain, and an eerie, discordant saxophone solo. Simon's lyrics, always cryptic, tip over into impenetrable; mull them over in your head as long as you can, letting them bounce around your brain, and you still won't ferret out what he's going on about. The accompanying video was directed by Simon Milne, a replacement for an over-taxed and overcommitted Russell Mulcahy. Like the song, it's a puzzle box, a mystery offering too few clues to allow anything more than a wild stab at a solution.

In the opening moments, Simon, John, and Roger trudge across a barren wasteland under a blazing sun (the video was filmed in Australia, the go-to locale for filmmakers in need of a suitably post-apocalyptic terrain). Nearby, a green-painted man sporting fangs and reptilian prosthetics slithers on all fours across the sand, which doesn't seem to alarm the Durans in the slightest; this is the kind of world where mutant snake-men don't merit a second glance. The Durans come across a pickup truck with a dead man in the front seat. John and Roger investigate, then succumb to exhaustion or some mystery ailment and slump to the ground.

Simon trails a mysterious brunette dressed as a sexy bellhop into a neglected church inside a candlelit subterranean lair, where he encounters Nick, who appears to be some kind of mystic or scholar, and Andy, who is doing nothing in particular. Nick pores over ancient scrolls and looks glamorous and ethereal while swaddled in eight billion yards of baggy tweed. No stranger to weird-ass outfits, Nick outdoes himself on a sartorial level in this video; his tweed ensemble—wide padded shoulders, shapeless cut, nubbly texture, matching slouchy trousers—might be the most baroquely bizarre item he's ever worn. It's sincerely, profoundly ugly, and yet strangely compelling. This is an outfit that could only be pulled off by someone who has crushed the musty conventions of fashion to powder beneath his dainty and expensively-shod feet.

Simon flees from the temple, pursued by a horde of feral lads in loincloths; unable to capture him, they battle amongst themselves in an acrobatic but ineffectual manner, which mostly involves taking balletic leaps into each other's arms. On the surface, pink neon rockets streak across the sky and detonate in the sand. While a revived John and Roger watch from the safety of the pickup truck, Simon staggers out of the lair and collapses in a heap. In the morning, he finds himself alone; Roger and John couldn't be bothered to rescue him before driving off, the rat bastards. He hitches a ride with a passing leggy brunette on horseback and gallops off into the horizon.

Yeah. I don't know what it all means, either.

Rumors abound that "Union of the Snake" was meant to be the first of an eventual series of interlinked videos, which makes sense; actually, that's about the only thing that does make sense about it. On the spectrum of Duran Duran videos, it tends to get overlooked, made redundant by the big-budget, bombastic video for "The Wild Boys," which would be released the following year. "Union of the Snake" contains many of the elements that would be repeated on a grander scale in "The Wild Boys": spooky subterranean lairs, mutants, a hazy yet pervasive sense of mysticism, paint-slathered feral boys running around without any pants on, and quasi-erotic hybrids of fighting and dancing, carried out by the aforementioned paint-slathered pantless feral boys.

"The Wild Boys" is Duran Duran's best song, I boldly proclaim, thus opening myself up to a deluge of impassioned criticism on the topic. I realize this argument is a hard sell. This is a song you don't so much sing as wail (save yourself some grief at karaoke night and opt to flex your pipes on "Hungry Like the Wolf" instead); you can hear the strain in Simon's voice on every note of that anguished chorus, with lyrics that invoke fire and murder and bloodstains. It's a full-throated, tormented blast of sound, backed up by urgent tribal drums and dramatic stings. It's dark and overwrought and perfect. I adore it and feel possessive of it, so much so that when John Taylor, in the 1987 documentary *Three To Get Ready*, refers to the pleasant yet inconsequential "Skin Trade" as "an infinitely better song than 'Wild Boys'," I was willing to challenge him to fisticuffs to defend its honor.

In its time, "The Wild Boys" was the most expensive music video ever made. The combined budget for it plus the full *Arena (An Absurd Notion)* concert film, of which the video was a key component, came in at over a million pounds. The video, shot over ten days at Shepperton Studios in Surrey, takes place entirely within a vast, dark, cavernous lair, lined with scaffolding and filled with a huge lagoon. It opens with a disembodied, moving animatronic head with a shaved skull and greying rubbery skin watching footage of the band on a bank of monitors. In the lair, the band members, dressed in tattered yet stylish *Mad Max*-inspired leather ensembles, are the captives of a band of feral young men, some of whom appear to be mutants, clad in loincloths and feathers. Simon is tied to a gigantic windmill, which dunks his head into the lagoon with each rotation. Andy is bound high up in the scaffolding, while Roger tools around the lair in his own little jet-powered hot air balloon. Nick is trapped in a cage; John is strapped down across the hood of a car, writhing around helplessly, forced to watch while monitors display images of his luminous face. If bondage is your fetish, "The Wild Boys" is your favorite Duran Duran video.

Simon has insisted the video is a metaphor for the trappings of mega-fame, which makes sense. The band members are evidently being forced to perform in captivity: Andy is clutching his guitar in the scaffolding, and Simon is singing his heart out while strapped to that ever-revolving windmill. It's not difficult to see parallels to Duran Duran's situation, in which their all-encompassing high-pressure global fame was starting to seem like a prison. On a metaphorical level, Simon's claim seems entirely plausible.

If we're talking *literally*, though... This is what the "Wild Boys" video is literally about: It's a prelude to a gang-bang.

Yeah. *That's* why the Durans are all in captivity.

Go back to the source material. See, Russell Mulcahy optioned the rights to the William S. Burroughs novella *The Wild Boys: A Book of the Dead* with an eye toward turning it into a full-length feature film, then asked Duran Duran to write a song for it. Mulcahy and the Durans weren't the first to turn to this particular source for inspiration; after all, David Bowie admitted that Ziggy Stardust and the Spiders from Mars were inspired directly by Burroughs's febrile imaginings. The book is a hallucinogenic fever dream, a frenzied tale of semi-mystical rampaging gangs of savage young men who frantically copulate with each other in a near-future dystopia. The song and the video serve as a teaser for the prospective film, which was never made, probably because mainstream audiences in 1984 weren't up for a big Hollywood movie about marauding teen boys engaging in frequent violent bouts of orgiastic gay sex, even while accompanied by a lively Duran Duran soundtrack.

Compared to the labyrinthine storyline of "Union of the Snake," not much happens in "The Wild Boys." After singing his heart out for a while, Simon eventually frees himself from the windmill and splashes around in the lagoon, and then he engages in combat with a multi-toothed albino mutant fish that tries to eat his face, and then he rescues his friends, maybe; the video sort of glosses over that part. It all ends with a ticker-tape parade, the five Durans cruising through the now-empty subterranean lair in a fancy vintage automobile, looking noble and glamorous while confetti rains down on them. The question lingers as to who is throwing the confetti; the chamber is now vacant, the pantless feral boys apparently having been vanquished in some part of the video we didn't get to see. The world as we knew it ended long ago, and all that remains are the beautiful boys of Duran Duran. Sounds about right.

CHAPTER TEN: ARENA, EXPLAINED

WHAT IS ARENA?

In terms of Duran Duran, *Arena* sometimes refers to the band's 1984 live album, which was recorded at the Oakland Coliseum during the Sing Blue Silver world tour. Here, though, it refers to *Arena (An Absurd Notion),* a science fiction-themed concert film directed by the band's frequent collaborator, Russell Mulcahy. *Arena* was mostly shot over the course of three performances in Oakland in April 1984; additional footage was also filmed at Shepperton Studios in Surrey and during a special free concert at the Birmingham National Exhibition Centre. It was released on VHS in 1985; an alternate version, recut to include additional songs and to remove the sci-fi elements, aired on Cinemax under the title *As the Lights Go Down.*

A science fiction-themed concert film?

Indeed. There's a framing device running throughout *Arena* concerning the band's namesake, *Barbarella*'s intergalactic ne'er-do-well Dr. Durand-Durand—played here, as in the original film, by the late Irish actor Milo O'Shea—who, after picking up a signal from Earth broadcasting the sound of thousands of young concert-goers chanting his name, heads to Oakland in anticipation of recapturing his former glory. Upon his arrival, he discovers the kids are actually screaming for a quintet of fluffy-haired pretty boys. As any self-respecting intergalactic ne'er-do-well would, he promptly swears dark vengeance upon Duran Duran for stealing his name, then tries to disrupt the concert through a series of diabolical schemes involving an army of armored dwarves, spike-toothed aquatic mutants who menace chained-up lingerie-clad roller derby dolls, and rubber-suited masked cyborgs who vigorously copulate in tanks of viscous green goo.

That sounds kinky. And awesome!

I know, right? Parts of *Arena* are indeed kinky and/or awesome. Parts of it are tedious and/or incomprehensible. Given near-limitless resources, Mulcahy stuffed *Arena* with ambitious, grandiose ideas, some of which are beautifully realized, and some of which veer into incoherence. The major problems with *Arena*, however, stem from timing. By this point, Duran Duran had been touring relentlessly for five months, a nearly unbroken stretch of concerts, promotion, and travel, all while coping with the rarified stresses that come from being preposterously famous. Exhausted and spread too thin, their participation was, by necessity, limited strictly to performing onstage. So while there's this elaborate and expansive framing device surrounding them, the Durans remain essentially untouched by it. As a result, there's a lot of distracting tonal dissonance between the Durand-Durand stuff and the Duran Duran stuff.

Is the Durand-Durand stuff any good?

The gorgeous opening sequence hits all the right cyber-punk/post-apocalyptic buttons; it's part *Blade Runner*, part *Mad Max Beyond Thunderdome*. Upon arriving on Earth, Durand-Durand, sporting a thick mustache and dark hair that render him nearly unrecognizable from his *Barbarella* days, wanders through the vast, cavernous bowels of the Coliseum, bellowing out for his welcoming party. He's walking around on four tall, skinny stilts attached to his arms and legs, with a helmeted, armored dwarf riding on his back. He situates himself in a control room, then summons an army of dwarves with cockney accents to do his evil bidding, i.e. disturbing the Durans as they perform overhead.

How's the concert footage?

Great, though you've seen it before—again, this is all part of the well-chronicled Sing Blue Silver tour, which was featured both in the video for "The Reflex" and, of course, in the concert documentary *Sing Blue Silver*. All the Durans look healthy and happy: Simon's got a great haircut, John's cheekbones won't quit, Nick is glacial and imperious, Roger keeps his head down and bangs on his drums, and Andy looks unkempt and semi-feral, but seems to be having a blast.

And then Durand-Durand tries to disrupt them?

In a roundabout way. He sends his armored dwarves to annoy the concertgoers, who seem remarkably unconcerned by their efforts. As Simon sings "Hungry Like the Wolf," a tiger prowls through the crowd, though it's unclear whether that's Durand-Durand's handiwork as well. The tiger keeps changing into a sexy bathing suit-clad lady, then back into a tiger. Simon wanders off the stage and finds himself at a spooky Aztec temple, which is teeming with: a) tigers, and b) sexy women dressed up like tigers.

Tigers? Wouldn't wolves make more sense for "Hungry Like the Wolf"?

Probably, but this tour was supporting the *Seven and the Ragged Tiger* album, after all. And ever since Sheila Ming turned into a cheetah in the "Hungry Like the Wolf" video, this song has been inextricably linked with jungle cats. Duran Duran have always been keen on big cats: According to his ex-wife, Nick originally wanted to have live panthers roaming around their wedding reception. (You'll be relieved yet faintly disappointed to hear sanity prevailed, and he settled for live flamingos instead.) More recently, on 2011's *All You Need Is Now* album, the band gave the world "The Man Who Stole a Leopard," a heartrendingly gorgeous song about fucking a leopard.

Wait, literally?

Yep. At the start of the song, it seems like the lyrics are metaphorical, like Simon is comparing a slinky, seductive woman to an animal, and then there's a reveal at the end where it becomes clear the song's narrator is actually, er, romantically entangled with a leopard. Great song, though. Possibly the most lushly romantic number about bestiality ever written.

What's Duran Duran's deal with women turning into animals?

It's a little much, right? I'd like to think this sort of blithe, brainless sexism was just a product of the time. Images of sexy women turning into sexy animals seem quintessentially eighties somehow, all part of the requisite trappings of oversexed yuppies, along with *Penthouse* subscriptions, Nagel prints, and framed posters of garages filled with Ferraris. The five Durans, being a pack of wealthy, horny twentysomethings, would have been exactly the right demographic to find this sort of nonsense appealing. Then I remember that "The Man Who Stole a Leopard" was released in 2011.

I don't know. It's problematic, I'll say that.

Back to *Arena*: "Hungry Like the Wolf" ends, and Duran Duran launch into "Union of the Snake." Somewhere offstage, a pair of sleek masked cyborgs copulate in a vat of green goo.

What do the cyborgs have to do with Durand-Durand's plan?

Couldn't tell you. Maybe Durand-Durand wanted to use them to thwart the Durans in some way, but they got distracted and started having sex instead. Fair enough.

Apart from performing onstage, do any of the Durans other than Simon have anything to do?

During "Save a Prayer," John leaves the stage and lurks in a corridor, where he bats his eyes at a super cute young fan while knocking back a mid-concert Heineken. It's possibly the most effective moment of product placement of all time, because it makes me *really* want a Heineken.

Did Heineken promptly recruit John Taylor to star in an advertising campaign?

No, and the world is a much grimmer place for that. Seeing John, sweaty and sultry, slurping down a Heineken backstage is one of the most brazenly erotic sights ever committed to film. He pants out a breathy greeting to the cute fan, then gets summoned by a roadie to go onstage and, like, do his job. Just before John returns to the stage, the fan gets grabbed a mysterious shadowy force, which drags her away, screaming, into the bowels of the Coliseum.

Does John notice?

Not so much, no. A vague expression of worry flickers over his beautiful face at the sound of her screams, then he shrugs and rejoins the in-progress concert. The next time we see the girl, Durand-Durand has locked her in a dangling cage in his underground lair.

Then we get to see the souped-up extended version of the "Wild Boys" video, which is the clear showpiece of *Arena*.

What's different about the extended version?

In a word: breasts.

Really? There are breasts in *The Wild Boys*?

We're talking about Duran Duran. Naturally, they managed to sneak some bare breasts into it. In the extended version, there's a topless Wild Girl, played by dancer/actor/former Billy Idol paramour Perri Lister. There are also some big explosions, some special effects that haven't held up especially well over the past thirty-odd years, and more footage of Simon strapped to that windmill. None of it is necessary, but it's a great video, so having even more of it is certainly a positive thing.

You said something about lingerie-clad roller derby dolls?

Right. While Duran Duran perform "Girls on Film," Durand-Duran's dwarves drag terrified female concert-goers off in nets. Next thing you know, the fans are skating madly around a roller derby rink while dressed in lacy lingerie, stockings, and dog collars. Simon, who is having a heck of a time remaining in one place during this concert, wanders offstage and ends up in the rink; the derby dolls kiss him and punch him in the face before he saunters back onto the stage and continues singing, wholly unfazed by all this.

Back in the rink, burly leather-clad masked dudes wielding bullwhips battle the derby dolls, who put up a good fight. This sort of cheerfully lurid S&M-tinged nonsense is operating right within Duran Duran's comfort zone. Thanks to Durand-Durand's interference, the women end up dangling upside-down in chains in the subterranean lair while being lowered slowly into fish tanks containing bald, spike-toothed, quasi-human creatures submerged in brackish fluid, breathing through an elaborate system of tubes and wires. It's both organic and mechanistic, the essence of cyberpunk writ large. Somewhere in Canada, William Gibson has a woody, and he doesn't know why.

Do Duran Duran rescue their fans?

No. First they'd have to notice their fans were in trouble.

Instead, while Duran Duran perform a spirited rendition of "The Reflex," a group of spunky young fans flood the underground lair and save the roller derby dolls from their weird fate.

Academy Award-winning actress Jennifer Connelly is in this, isn't she? Is she one of these fans?

That's a persistent rumor, but no, Connelly is not in *Arena*. She does appear briefly in *As the Lights Go Down*, which is the altered version of *Arena* that aired on Cinemax: She strolls languidly across the stage while Simon wails "Seventh Stranger," a song that is not included in *Arena*.

She's also one of the white-robed children in the temple in the "Union of the Snake" video, isn't she?

Nope. That's another persistent rumor with no truth to it.

But she *is* the fashion model Nick is photographing in the "View To a Kill" video, right?

Still no. That's Gail Elliot, who was fellow model Yasmin Le Bon's maid of honor at her wedding to Simon. Look, Jennifer Connelly doesn't need to be in *Arena*, or in "Union of the Snake." Connelly appeared with Duran Duran in *As the Lights Go Down* when she was fourteen, then starred with David Bowie in *Labyrinth* when she was sixteen. That's enough of a charmed life for any teen girl in the eighties. Anything more than that would just be excessive and ludicrous.

In the lair, the spunky fans defeat Durand-Durand via a spirited synchronized dance number and strategic use of a gigantic Duran Duran poster.

That sounds kind of...

The word you're probably looking for is "crappy," though "lame" is also acceptable. Coming on the tail end of some fabulous visuals and some entertainingly bonkers plot twists, the climax is a whopping disappointment.

Durand-Durand staggers through the lair on his stilts and shoots flames from his mouth at the fans, who use the aforementioned Duran Duran poster to direct the fire right back at him. Ablaze, he tumbles off the stilts as the lair explodes around him. "I only wanted to be loved!" he howls. Credits roll over the lively strains of "Rio."

Is that... it?

Yeah, pretty much. Again, *Arena*'s fatal flaw is simply that, apart from performing onstage, the band members don't get anything to do, remaining largely untouched while all this berserk chaos surrounds them. Simon ogles tiger-women and gets assaulted by roller derby dolls, and John makes sweet, sweet love to a can of Heineken, and that's it. It's not enough. Because the Durans aren't integrated into the action, the entire Durand-Durand plotline, as cool as some of it is, ends up seeing like an unnecessary distraction.

Overall, though, is *Arena* worth it?

Yes. Yes. A thousand times, yes. Sure, at times *Arena* seems less like a concert film and more like a cry for help; watching *Arena* in all its bizarre incoherence will tax the patience of all but the most fervent Duran Duran fan. Still, though, at its core, there's something compulsively fascinating about it. I own another Duran Duran concert film on DVD, the straightforward and tasteful *Live at Hammersmith '82!*; I've watched it maybe twice. I've probably seen *Arena* close to twenty, maybe thirty times, and I still feel like I've barely scratched the surface of its madness. You know that concert film Duran Duran made with David Lynch? It can't hold a candle to *Arena*'s freeform weirdness.

David Lynch directed a Duran Duran concert film?

That'd be *Duran Duran Unstaged*, featuring footage from the band's 2011 All You Need Is Now tour, which was released on DVD in 2013. Lynch superimposes footage of random crap—creepy clay heads, hot dogs sizzling on a grill, that kind of thing—over images of the band performing.

And it's less strange than this?

It's downright tame by comparison. If for no other reason than managing to out-weird David Lynch, Russell Mulcahy should be proud of what he's achieved with *Arena*.

CHAPTER ELEVEN: ONCE IS A COCTEAU TRIBUTE, TWICE IS A FETISH

IN LATE 1984, Duran Duran committed the pop-music equivalent of cellular mitosis by temporarily dividing into two separate bands: Andy and John teamed up with blue-eyed soul singer Robert Palmer and drummer Tony Thompson of the funk-soul band Chic to form the Power Station, while Simon, Nick, and Roger became Arcadia. The two new bands were dissimilar fraternal twins, sharing hefty parts of Duran Duran's DNA yet looking and sounding nothing alike. Having felt marginalized by the synth-dominant sound of *Seven and the Ragged Tiger*, John and Andy wanted to create something harder, faster, closer to true rock. Mission accomplished: Listening to the Power Station is akin to staggering around in a coked-up blur, careening from club to club, wobbling on too-high heels while laughing your ass off at nothing in particular. Whatever else it may be, it's rock. It's definitely rock.

The Power Station's self-titled album, produced by Chic legend Bernard Edwards, pulses and crackles with frenetic energy. The album cover features a topless woman drawn in broad red strokes against a black background. She could be a bastardized version of one of Patrick Nagel's iconic women, reduced to her most basic lines: electric squiggles for her hair, circles for her breasts, dots for her nipples. She's featureless apart from her mouth, which is open and red and waiting. An animated neon version of the Power Station's dream girl dances and writhes her way through the video for their debut single, "Some Like It Hot"; midway through the video she's brought to life in the statuesque form of six-foot transgender model Tula. Tula wears neon-green eye shadow and neon-pink lipstick, which matches the neon-pink cones of her strapless bustier; she bathes beneath a sun lamp next to a neon-orange cactus in the middle of a scorching desert under an electric blue sky. "Some Like It Hot" doesn't just heat up its surroundings, it burns everything it touches to cinders.

The Power Station scored two monster hits off their album, following up "Some Like It Hot" with a revved-up cover of the T-Rex hit "Bang a Gong (Get It On)," which they renamed, in the apparent interest of causing widespread confusion and preventing easy cataloguing, "Get It On (Bang a Gong)." (In the Power Station's slight defense, the song's true original title is simply "Get It On"; T-Rex was forced to change it for the US market to differentiate it from a similarly-titled tune.) In the summer of 1985, the Power Station went on tour in the United States to support the album, though by that point Palmer had already left the band to pursue a solo career; he was replaced by Michael Des Barres. Capitalizing on their brief time in the spotlight, the Power Station performed on *Saturday Night Live*; they also made an appearance on an episode of *Miami Vice*, in which John giggles and slurs his way through a couple of lines of dialogue before taking the stage with his bandmates to play a blistering rendition of "Get It On (Bang a Gong)." Or maybe they play "Bang a Gong (Get It On)." It's hard to tell.

Next to the Power Station's scorching heat, the boys of Arcadia were detached, remote, frosty. They were *artsy*. So very artsy. Their album, *So Red the Rose*, featured guest vocals from Sting, guitar work by Pink Floyd's David Gilmour, and a spoken-word interval from Grace Jones. They took their name from a seventeenth-century Nicolas Poussin painting, *Et in Arcadia Ego*, a mannered composition of shepherds in a field examining an inscription on a tombstone. If the Power Station is a fevered, cocaine-fueled bender, Arcadia is an opium haze, a visit to a surreal and hazardous dreamland filled with beautiful and unfathomable creatures. Nick and Simon (and, to a reduced extent, Roger) burst forth in brand-new images to suit their new project: unnaturally pale skin, heavily lined eyes, darkly painted lips. They were Goth before Goth took hold as a cultural moment; they dyed their hair the color of a starless void and darkened their eyebrows to match.

Perhaps the most famous photo shoot from the Arcadia era features Nick and Simon—hair blackened, eyebrows fierce, makeup flawless—posing together in tuxedos. In some shots, they're clutching bouquets of red roses; in others, they're clutching each other, Nick's head resting softly against Simon's shoulder, like they're posing for the school photographer at Vampire Prom. They're playing around with the imagery of romance, pantomiming a courtship to spark interest in their side project. It's all done with a flirty, self-aware wink, but it speaks to a bigger point about Arcadia. Duran Duran is and always has been a democracy, with equal representation from all members, but Simon, as the frontman, is the band's public face, the figure in the spotlight at the center of the stage, the one who seizes the biggest, juiciest role in all their music videos. Arcadia, though, was a partnership between Simon and Nick; the spotlight expanded to accommodate them both.

Not Roger, though. By this point, the spotlight was Roger's enemy. He appears in none of Arcadia's videos; he skipped many of the photo shoots as well.

The video for Arcadia's "Goodbye is Forever" was directed by Marcelo Anciano, who'd assisted Russell Mulcahy on several earlier Duran Duran videos. It's a Maxfield Parrish painting in a steampunk setting, following Nick and Simon on a breezy, bucolic idyll through the inner workings of a clock. At some points in the video, they appear to be captives, caged or in bondage, while at other times they're free to roam around; at no point are they ever fazed by the strangeness of their predicament. There's a languid, gentle, dreamlike quality to it, which suits the song. Arcadia's songs are dense and cerebral (the word "pretentious" gets tossed around a lot in discussions about Arcadia), filled with odd chord structures and atypical tempos. For the most part, they're not especially hooky.

"Election Day," Arcadia's first single and its only top-ten hit, is *almost* hooky. At the very least, I hum a few bars of it whenever I'm standing in line at my local polling place waiting to cast a vote. It's a seductive, slithery, ominous song, filled with a sense of existential dread; it's not clear what it all means, but when Simon purrs out lyrics about how it's coming up on re-election day, there's probably cause to worry about the ballot results.

The video for "Election Day" was directed by Roger Christian, the Oscar-winning set designer of *Star Wars*, who was a last-minute replacement for Ridley Scott, believe it or not, the prolific and revered director known for game-changing genre films like *Alien* and *Blade Runner*, who dropped out of the project to work on 1985's *Legend*. I'd say Scott made entirely the wrong choice—the "Election Day" video is something close to art, whereas *Legend* is filled with unicorns galloping around sunlit fields in slow motion to a Tangerine Dream soundtrack, like a *Saturday Night Live* parody of a tampon commercial—but then I remember the good bits, such as Tim Curry's splendidly villainous turn as the Lord of Darkness, or a long-haired Tom Cruise scampering about like a disco gladiator in a sparkly gold tunic and no pants. Nevertheless, "Election Day" is the better, weirder project.

For "Election Day," Nick and Simon ramp up their proto-Goth images another few notches. They look awesome and villainous, with eyebrows like matched pairs of black caterpillars wriggling across their pale, powdered foreheads. Simon wears a flowing black coat; Nick's in a boxy suit complete with black satin gloves and a walking stick. His jet-black hair bursts out in feather-soft face-framing spikes and cascades down his back; it's... well, it's clearly a mullet, but a fancy one, so let's give it a fancy French pronunciation: moo-LAY. Nick doesn't have a mullet, he has a *moolay*.

It's a sinister video. Nick and Simon arrive together at a decadent, decaying party, where many of the sleek, glamorous guests appear to be drugged or dead. They split up and explore the venue; Simon nuzzles with a succession of leggy brunettes in tight dresses while Nick clutches a lit candelabra and slithers along dark corridors. An aura of cold malevolence infuses everything, from the stilted and peculiar dance routine the party guests spontaneously break into, to the cluster of well-dressed women playing a lethal dice game with crystals, to the sculpted shirtless men loitering around menacingly while wearing horse masks. Of the latter, Simon and Nick claim it's a tribute to *Testament of Orpheus*, the 1960 film by legendary Surrealist Jean Cocteau, which also featured a man-horse hybrid. They're right, of course, though it's worth pointing out that this is not the first time a shirtless man in a horse mask has factored into a Duran Duran (or, in Arcadia's case, a Duran-adjacent) video. It's possible the oiled-down masked dude giving the cowgirl a pony ride in "Girls on Film" was meant as a Cocteau tribute, too, though it seems equally possible—nay, probable—that this is some kind of Duran-specific fetish, right up there with sexy women transforming into sexy cats.

Arcadia's final video, "The Flame," was directed by Russell Mulcahy, in what would turn out to be his final collaboration with Duran Duran. "The Flame" is a stylish homage to English parlor mysteries; Agatha Christie would nod in recognition at many of the elements, the sinister butler and the poisoned soup and the disapproving dowagers. There's a hefty dollop of *The Rocky Horror Picture Show* thrown in for good measure, with Nick serving as a demure and elegant Dr. Frank-N-Furter to Simon's nebbish Brad Majors. Simon, kitted out in full nerd regalia—glasses, bowtie, sweater vest— arrives at a spooky, lavish mansion on a foggy evening, where he's invited to join a dinner party hosted by Nick, the stylish young lord of the manor. Homicidal mayhem ensues.

For unknown reasons, various party guests repeatedly attempt to murder Simon; Nick, a poised and polished force of benevolent malice, alternates between mocking him and saving his hide. At the video's end, Nick and Simon, along with Nick's chic female companion, slink away arm in arm, leaving behind a mansion filled with dead guests.

"The Flame" ends on a freeze-frame and a title card proclaiming "To Be Continued," which is a cruel tease; more than thirty years have passed, and Simon and Nick have yet to revisit this world. Arcadia dissolved away, once again becoming part of Duran Duran, while Andy and John left the smoking embers of the Power Station behind as well. The original members of the Power Station reunited for a new album and a tour in 1996, though the project ended grimly. John dropped out early on and was replaced by Bernard Edwards, who died suddenly of pneumonia before the tour's start; Tony Thompson and Robert Palmer both died, too young and too damn early, in 2003. Only Duran Duran endures.

CHAPTER TWELVE: JEUX D'ESPIONS

JOHN TAYLOR USED to date a Bond girl, *Octopussy*'s Janine Andrews. He also once claimed he'd like to play James Bond, which is in some ways a capital suggestion; the man knows how to pose in a tuxedo, and there's much to be said for an incarnation of Bond with razors for cheekbones and a lush thatch of glossy hair. While John has dabbled in acting over the past few decades— standout roles include the prehistoric Keith Richards ("Keith Rockhard") to Alan Cumming's Mick Jagger ("Mick Jagged") in *The Flintstones in Viva Rock Vegas* and a billionaire rapist-slash-murderer in *Vegas: City of Dreams*, a straight-to-video tit flick with an incongruous Christian bent—it seems increasingly unlikely he'll ever be Bond. But it's all thanks to his Bond obsession that we ended up with the greatest Bond theme of all time.

I don't say that lightly. There have been some mighty fine Bond themes over the years, and I wouldn't want to slight exceptional songs like Shirley Bassey's "Goldfinger" and Adele's "Skyfall." For sheer unexpurgated awesomeness, though, it's tough to top Duran Duran's "A View to a Kill."

As legend has it, John approached Bond producer Albert R. "Cubby" Broccoli at a party and suggested Duran Duran provide the theme for his upcoming film. Because it was 1985 and Duran Duran had the ability to move the universe with simple requests, Broccoli agreed. The band, still fractured into two ragged and exhausted camps from the Arcadia-Power Station split, returned to the studio to write and record the song, working closely with longtime Bond composer John Barry.

Magic happened. "A View to a Kill" is both haunting and exhilarating, filled with dramatic stings and evocative images of crystal tears that fall like snowflakes on bodies. It's wonderful.

That video, though.

Duran Duran reunited with Kevin Godley and Lol Creme, the directing team behind "Girls on Film," to shoot "A View to a Kill." The video, which would be the final one made by all five original band members until 2003's "(Reach Up for the) Sunrise," is constructed of equal parts brilliance and crap. Set at the Eiffel Tower, it features an irresistible, impossible-to-beat premise, in which the Durans play a quintet of glamorous spies carrying out lethal missions, intercut with matching film footage in which Roger Moore's James Bond tangles with an assassin played by Grace Jones.

Delightful idea, right? Only it doesn't work, not really. On a purely technical level, there's a visual mismatch between the film footage and the video footage, but that's small potatoes; a bigger issue is how the end result is marred by some out-of-place goofiness. Do yourself a favor and stop watching before the tag ending, in which Simon delivers the line, "Bon. Simon Le Bon," to a French fan with wholly unwarranted smugness. You just murdered your own video, Simon; there's no need to look cocky about it.

The band is separated into two groups of spies, divided by their recent side projects: John and Andy (Team Power Station) face off against Simon, Nick, and Roger (Team Arcadia) in a deadly duel. This is a conceptual goldmine! Just the thought of it is enough to give me a frisson of excitement.

But "A View to a Kill" reflects a band in crisis. Discord bleeds through the screen. The band members are filmed in isolation; apart from two brief wide-angle shots that manage to include both Nick and Andy, no Durans share any screen time with each other. The production was well-documented by a journalist from *People* magazine who was on the set writing an article about the band, so it's clear Simon, John, Nick, Roger, and Andy all worked on the video at the same time, but you'd never know that from the finished product.

Enter Simon, secret agent extraordinaire, skulking around an observation deck. He's clad in a white trench coat over Breton stripes, paired with a beret at a jaunty angle, and he looks goddamned amazing, like he's in Paris to shoot a spread for *Vogue Hommes*. He's using his Sony Walkman as a remote detonator to blow up stuff. At the push of a button, a helicopter explodes in Antarctica; another button causes a blimp to crash into the Golden Gate Bridge. Simon is carrying out orders given to him through his headphones by Roger, the clear mastermind of Team Arcadia, who is sitting amidst a sea of high-tech surveillance equipment in a command center in the back of a catering van (the van is emblazoned with "Chez Tayloire," because this video is a little zany). Roger monitors the action at the Eiffel Tower and gives commands by phone to Nick and Simon.

Holy smokes, Roger looks unwell. He's lit with harsh overhead lights, which isn't going to make anyone look healthy and well-rested, but he has dark slashes beneath his eyes, his skin looks gray, and he seems dispirited and exhausted to his core. He's running on fumes. The joy of being a Duran has long since drained from Roger; every time I watch this video, I feel a strong urge to draw him a hot bath and fix him a nice cup of tea.

On the Eiffel Tower, Nick takes stealth surveillance photos while undercover as a fashion photographer. He's retained his Arcadia hairdo—he's still sporting a formidable *moolay*—though he's switched the color from jet black to an ashy, streaky blond. His face is impeccably painted (as detailed in that aforementioned *People* article, he's sporting "plum blush, black eye pencil and liner by Clinique and coral lipstick by Christian Dior"),[10] and he looks like a star. Over on Team

Power Station, John saunters around the observation deck while looking inhumanly beautiful, which is something he does very well.

Andy, John's partner in subterfuge, poses as a blind accordion player, complete with dark glasses and a cane. His hair is a huge, gloriously tangled mess; odds are good he's got a litter of newborn kittens living in there. Andy, it seems, no longer has time or use for Duran Duran's polished and well-coiffed public image; from here on out, he's going to be doing his own thing, style-wise, and his own thing is going to involve dumping kerosene on his hairbrush and setting it on fire. When he spots Nick secretly photographing John, he presses a special button on his accordion, which causes Nick's camera to explode. Nick goes down screaming in a blast of flame.

Ouch. Unless I've missed something, this is the sole instance of Duran-on-Duran violence in a Duran Duran video. This video just turned into a Duran Duran snuff film.

"A View to a Kill" marks the end of an era, the decline of the Golden Age of Duran, a slide that was anticipated the previous year by the formation of the Power Station and Arcadia. The song is released in May of 1985; in July, Duran Duran perform it in Philadelphia at Live Aid, in what turns out to be the last time all five band members appear onstage together until 2003. Live Aid is a huge global event, a continent-spanning televised music festival to raise money for famine relief in Ethiopia, but it's an ignominious sendoff for Duran Duran's glorious original lineup. They're exhausted and under-rehearsed, and Simon's voice hits a wonky note midway through the song in front of a live television audience of close to two billion viewers. By their willing admission, they have a pretty rotten time onstage that day. The wild ride is over.

CHAPTER THIRTEEN: MELANCHOLIA

ROGER LEAVES FIRST, exhausted and shaken from years in the spotlight. Being a thoughtful, conscientious sort, he takes pains to preserve his professional and personal relationships with his bandmates, and he exits Duran Duran with all bridges still standing. Andy takes off shortly thereafter; he burns his bridges, then torches the surrounding village for good measure. It's an acrimonious split, resulting in prolonged legal battles, mudslinging in the press, and hurt feelings on all sides, and when it's all over, Duran Duran are a three-man band.

As it shakes out, Roger and Andy are expendable, barely. Fans are distraught at the news, but they mostly remain loyal. It's a staggering blow, yet not a mortal one. Duran Duran are able to forge ahead.

Duran Duran's first album post-split is 1986's *Notorious*, their first studio album since 1983's *Seven and the Ragged Tiger*. They team up with Nile Rodgers, co-founder of Chic and music producer extraordinaire. They'd collaborated with him before on "The Reflex" and "The Wild Boys" and had gravitated toward his style; they trust him to work his magic on the album. With Rodgers's guidance, they cultivate a new sound, something a little more infused with funk, with rock, with soul. It's the right move. The second half of the eighties is upon them, and things have changed, and Duran Duran must adapt or get left behind.

Notorious is a success, more or less. Peak Duran, that golden stretch from 1982 to 1985 when the band could do no wrong, is now in the past; they'll never capture that level of global hysteria again. By the standards of Peak Duran, maybe *Notorious* is a disappointment. By any reasonable measure, though, it does fine. Critics like it; people buy it. It's a good album.

But it's a different world for Duran Duran now. Everything about the band hit maximum levels in 1985: Their hairstyles couldn't get any larger, their videos couldn't get any more extravagant, their fans couldn't scream any louder. Now, by necessity, Duran Duran have to reign it in. They become smaller and quieter, which is a natural enough progression; there are fewer Durans now, for one thing. The hysteria has ebbed. Nick chops off his glorious mullet; it will never again make an appearance.

Their videos, too, get smaller and quieter. Duran Duran release three singles from *Notorious*, the title track plus "Skin Trade" and "Meet El Presidente." The videos for each are uniformly muted. No yachts, no zombies, no exotic locales, no post-apocalyptic wastelands, no murders. No bare breasts, no sexy women turning into sexy animals. All the *Notorious*-era videos are variations on a single theme; they all feature artistic, stylish footage of the band performing, often interspersed with shots of beautiful women. That's pretty much it. Duran Duran are incapable of disappointing me, exactly; being disappointed by Duran Duran is like being disappointed that the unicorn in your front yard isn't as sparkly as you'd hoped. Still, for the first time ever, Duran Duran seem capable of being... well, maybe a little bit boring.

Just as the giddy, high-volume hysteria of *Sing Blue Silver* captured the essence of Peak Duran, a documentary about *Notorious*-era Duran reflects this more sedate period. Directed by David Gasperik, *Three to Get Ready* follows Simon, John, and Nick around Los Angeles in early 1987 while they do publicity for their upcoming Strange Behaviour tour. *Three to Get Ready* is less juicy and endlessly quotable than *Sing Blue Silver*, but it's *good*, particularly for the slice-of-Duran-life aspect. Watch it for the scene in which the Durans hash out the details of their tour rider ("*French* champagne," Nick specifies, with the injured look of someone whose palate has been contaminated backstage by subpar domestic plonk one too many times. "No obscure cheeses!" John adds).

They've lost valuable ground. They're still world famous, sure, but they've fallen from the pinnacle, and they know it. In *Three to Get Ready*, we see a rare trace of skittishness in their interactions with the press. They're gun-shy in advance of an appearance on *The Late Show*, hosted by Joan Rivers; Joan wants them to sit down for an interview after performing, which they all agree is a bad idea, because they've taken some knocks in the press lately. Despite their best efforts, Joan effortlessly maneuvers them over to her couch post-performance for some chitchat. Joan Rivers, 1. Durans, 0. They talk in mournful terms about the runaway success of U2, then blazing up the charts with "With or Without You." They field a barrage of threatened legal proceedings from Andy; when their lawyer brings them the latest missive from their estranged bandmate, he cheerfully refers to it as "this week's Andy Taylor lawsuit." All is not well in Duranville.

If *Notorious* is a faint disappointment, their next album, 1988's *Big Thing* continues the gentle downhill slide. It starts off well, scoring a pair of low-key hits with its first two singles, "I Don't Want Your Love" and "All She Wants Is." The latter song comes complete with a visually striking stop-motion video directed by acclaimed artist Dean Chamberlain, who uses a sophisticated technique combining moving light sources and slow-frame photography to create an illusion of "drawing" pictures on film with light. After a promising start, *Big Thing* hits a rut when a third single, "Do You Believe in Shame?", goes nowhere on the charts. Part of this may have something to do with a controversy that arises over the songwriting credits: The melody of "Do You Believe in Shame?" bears a hard-to-overlook similarity to the Creedence Clearwater Revival hit, "Susie Q." The discovery of this similarity results in legal challenges and an eventual adjustment to the songwriting credits.

Lack of chart success notwithstanding, "Do You Believe in Shame?" is an exquisite song, steeped in melancholy. Simon writes it while grieving the untimely death of a close friend, David Miles; the song becomes the first of a trilogy of what he will later refer to as his "death songs" (rounding out the trio are "Ordinary World" off of 1993's *Wedding Album*, and "Out of My Mind" off of 1997's *Medazzaland*). The song is a desolate gut punch about death and grief, and it's got a bleak and beautiful video to match.

The video for "Do You Believe in Shame?" is the work of Chinese auteur Chen Kaige, who would go on to acclaim in the United States for directing *Farewell My Concubine*. In the video, Simon, Nick, and John—all looking wraithlike and unwell, like they're desperately in need of sunlight, fresh air, and a hearty dinner— wander around New York in numb states of grief, barely able to function. Simon breaks off his key in the lock of his apartment building; John gets caught in a revolving door. Nick, gaunt and weary, buys up various expensive tchotchkes at the auction of an artist's estate, then bundles them up and dumps them in a public trash bin; it's a clear reference to the recent death of his mentor, Andy Warhol. (Warhol chronicled his long-running friendship with Nick in his posthumously-released diaries; of his protégée, he once told *The Face* magazine, "I love him, I worship him. I masturbate to Duran Duran videos,"[11] thus showing that the twentieth century's most influential pop artist knew how to craft one heck of a memorable soundbite.)

DURANALYSIS

By video's end, the three Durans sit in a stark, bare apartment, frail and drained, watching dominos fall into endless coils. This is what grief is: emptiness and solitude, all while feeling like your soul has been obliterated by a nuclear blast. It's 1988, and this smaller, quieter, more introspective version of Duran Duran knows how to grieve.

CHAPTER FOURTEEN: EXTRAORDINARY WORLD

DURAN DURAN'S MIDAS touch vanishes with the eighties. After five years of soft yet noticeable decline, they have their first disaster with their 1990 album, *Liberty*. They're a five-man team again, having hired two new permanent(ish) members: guitarist Warren Cuccurullo, formerly of Missing Persons, who has performed with Duran Duran on an unofficial basis since Andy's departure, and drummer Sterling Campbell. *Liberty* produces two singles, both of which disappoint. "Violence of Summer" is half of a good song, with a lively video featuring a robust slice of rural Americana as envisioned by a bunch of glamorous English lads; in it, a gaggle of leggy models in bras and Brigitte Bardot wigs cavort around the countryside, channeling the spirit of Anna Nicole Smith's campaign for Guess. It's... fine, I suppose. The video for their second single, "Serious," comes straight from the *Notorious* playbook; it features black-and-white footage of the band performing while model Tess Daly, future *Strictly Come Dancing* host, stands around and looks beautiful. "Serious" fails to make any impact on the charts; *Liberty* is a critical and commercial bust. For Duran Duran, the nineties are off to a shaky start.

By 1991, I've left Spokane for Los Angeles. I'm a student in the screenwriting program at USC's film school; I have a mailbox with my name on it in the George Lucas Building, which gives me a thrill every time I see it. The eighties are dead at this point, and I'm the only one who seems to mourn them. Within a few days of my arrival in L.A., Nirvana's "Smells Like Teen Spirit" dominates the radio waves, and from that point on, grunge is everywhere. Grunge disdains glamour; grunge is nihilistic and angsty. Grunge is an explicit rejection of Duran Duran and everything they stand for. Duran Duran are too inextricably linked to the colorful excesses of the eighties to reinvent themselves as part of grunge's drab milieu; they'd be fools to even try. All Duran Duran can do is forge ahead, making their kind of music and waiting for the pendulum to swing back in their direction.

I don't like film school very much, which shocks me to my core. As it turns out, I'm a mediocre student in a mediocre program. My screenplays are impractical; my student films are half-assed. I'm poor, so the federal government is picking up the tab for my tuition, and I'm afraid it's not getting a good return on its investment. I am disaffected, jaded, unhappy. I complain a lot. Many people find me insufferable; they probably have a point. I've accepted that the eighties are gone, so I adjust my music tastes accordingly. A dude in my Comparative

Literature class tells me I look like I listen to a lot of Depeche Mode. I do, and I have the haircut and shitty attitude to prove it.

Duran Duran fall off my radar. The first time I hear "Ordinary World," I fail to recognize it as a Duran Duran song.

"Ordinary World" becomes a huge hit for the band. It's the first single off their self-titled 1993 album, which everybody always calls *The Wedding Album,* because Duran Duran already released a self-titled album back in 1981 and one should be plenty for any band, even one as hilariously excessive as this one. It's a dreamy, optimistic, contemplative song, and, apart from Simon's very distinctive vocals, it Does. Not. Sound. Like. Duran. Duran. It sails up the charts, hitting number one on *Billboard*'s Top 40. They follow it up with another big hit, the sinuous and sleek "Come Undone."

They're now down to four members, Sterling Campbell having drifted away after the failure of *Liberty.* Warren is still a mainstay, one with ever-growing influence; he and Nick get along famously. Warren is a polarizing figure in the Duran Duran fandom, then and now, but he'll always be more or less okay in my book, thanks to his pre-Duran band, Missing Persons, whose song "Walking in L.A." becomes my personal anthem. "Walking in L.A." speaks to my soul. I will live in Los Angeles from 1991 to 2011 without ever once owning a car. I walk vast, huge, unfathomable distances, from my mid-Wilshire apartment to the beach, to the Hollywood

Hills, to downtown, to Pasadena. I become a running sight gag, because Missing Persons sing the truth: Nobody walks in L.A. Strangers approach me in grocery stores or in line at coffee shops: Didn't I see you walking...? I cut them off: Yes. Yes, you did. Wherever you saw me, that was me. I am the person who walks in L.A.

I graduate from film school and get a good job on a good television show. A few years later, I end up with a bad job on a bad television show. And then, for a distressingly lengthy stretch, I have no job at all. I make a lot of dubious career decisions.

So do Duran Duran. The boys follow up the unexpected chart-topping success of *The Wedding Album* with 1995's *Thank You*, an album of cover songs. There are gems on there—their version of Lou Reed's "Perfect Day" is pristine, their version of Grandmaster Melle Mel's "White Lines" becomes a new classic—and then there's their cover of Public Enemy's "911 Is a Joke." Twenty years later, comedians are *still* getting mileage out of that one; John Oliver uses it as a punch line in a 2016 *Last Week Tonight* segment on the United States' failing 911 system. Whatever momentum Duran Duran had gained with the success of *The Wedding Album* vanishes.

The next album, 1997's *Medazzaland*, flops in the United States; their longtime label, Capitol Records/EMI, doesn't even bother releasing it in Europe. Here in 2017, *Medazzaland* has *still* never seen a European release. Duran Duran are dropped by EMI; they find a new home at Hollywood Records, but it's still a blow. There's nothing fun about rejection.

The crushing part of all this? *Medazzaland* is a jewel of an album, containing some of the band's best songs in years. "Out of My Mind," which pops up on the soundtrack for the big-budget disappointment *The Saint*, has an eerily appropriate title; it's one of those songs that gets a snakelike hold on your brain and won't let go. "Michael You've Got a Lot to Answer For" is a poignant, stripped-down ode to Simon's close friend, INXS frontman Michael Hutchence. "Big Bang Generation" is hooky as all hell. "Electric Barbarella" has a sound that hails back to the glory days of Peak Duran; the lyrics are an enthusiastic paean to fucking a sexy robot.

Ah, "Electric Barbarella." I'm delighted when I first hear the song, and when I first see the accompanying sexy robot-fucking video, because *this* is the Duran Duran I fell in love with, lo these many years ago. "Electric Barbarella" holds the distinction of reportedly being the first song available for purchase via digital download; the video holds the distinction of being banned from Canada's MuchMusic network on the grounds that it's "just not very tasteful."[12] This is true. It is not.

"Electric Barbarella," directed by renowned photographer and filmmaker Ellen von Unwerth, opens with Simon, Nick, and Warren industriously shopping for a sexy robot, for purposes of general carnal mayhem and light housekeeping. The robot, played by model Myka Dunkle, eventually rebels against her despicable human overlords, attacking and electrocuting Simon, Nick, and Warren.

Simon, Nick, and Warren. Hey, are we missing anyone here?

John drifts away from Duran Duran during *Medazzaland*. He's been sober for a few years, finally gaining control over the various addictions that dogged him since Duran Duran's golden era; he's a new person now, and that person no longer wants to be a Duran. That's it for the band, I think to myself when I hear the news. I feel pretty sure Duran Duran can't survive without him.

Newly divorced from his first wife, British television personality Amanda de Cadenet, John lives in Los Angeles. Rumor has it he's entered the newfangled field of internet dating; there's probably no truth to this, but it's an irresistible thought. I fixate on this: How bizarre would it be find yourself in some bar making first-date chitchat with John Taylor, owner of the face that sold millions of issues of *Tiger Beat*?

John dabbles in acting. He does some solo work. Along with Guns N' Roses' Duff McKagan and Matt Sorum, plus Steve Jones of the Sex Pistols, he joins a super-group, Neurotic Outsiders. They have a regular gig at the Viper Room on Sunset. I'm vaguely aware of this, though I never see him perform.

I write so, so many screenplays. I sell none of them. I work random jobs out of desperation, getting further and further away from the entertainment industry. I temp a lot. I get pretty good at manning a switchboard. I see my friends and former classmates working on shows, making deals, collecting awards. I change my official theme song. No longer "Walking in L.A.," it's now Morrissey's "We Hate It When Our Friends Become Successful."

Failure sucks. I can't catch a break. Neither can Duran Duran. Still moving forward, even without John, they release an album in 1998, *Pop Trash*, which is glittery and fun. They're still in there swinging, but *Pop Trash* flops. I see their name in the back pages of *L.A. Weekly*, playing small gigs at local clubs, and I feel a burst of something deep in my chest: *This is something that used to be very important to me.*

In 2001, the news breaks: Duran Duran, the original lineup, are reuniting. Warren is out; John and Roger and even prodigal son Andy are back. They're recording a new album, and then they're going on tour, and then everything's going to be exactly as it once was.

Duran Duran survived the nineties, and they're heading strong into the millennium. I'm not sure anyone could've predicted this. Except for Duran Duran; they probably always knew. Failure can only be a temporary state for Duran Duran. Now and forever, they always come back around.

CHAPTER FIFTEEN: NICK RHODES IS AGING NATURALLY, AND OTHER STRANGE FACTS ABOUT LATE-ERA DURAN

NICK RHODES IS not a fan of cosmetic surgery. Claiming a fear of knives, he's left his famous face untouched as he ages, which comes as a surprise; given his celebrated vanity and attention to his public image, one would've expected him to be constantly tweaking and pulling and tucking, availing himself of the full battery of services offered by medical science to preserve the illusion of eternal youth. Instead, he's accepted wrinkles; he's let his glorious mane of hair thin, as hair is wont to do with age.

This is not to suggest he's let himself go. Lord, no; never that. Nick is the creative director of GeneU, a state-of-the-art skincare clinic on Bond Street, staffed by intimi-datingly lovely technicians wearing sparkly silver smocks. Pricey and posh, GeneU uses DNA testing to determine the perfect individualized skincare regimen. Nick uses their products, and it shows; he's holding up well. He's never given up makeup, either, though he's toned it down over the years.

They look good, all the current Durans, John and Simon and Nick and Roger (we'll get to Andy in a moment). They're lean and agile. They wear well-tailored suits, usually in black, often with a faint sparkle. They look healthy, particularly for a bunch of fiftysomething rock stars, like they've been eating all the right foods and getting plenty of fresh air. None of the Durans smoke anymore; two of the Durans are sober. The other two— if you've guessed Simon and Nick, give yourself an éclair—travel with an extensive portable wine cellar that fits in their private jet whenever the band goes on tour, because they're Duran Duran, damn it, and therefore have high standards of inaccessible glamour and dizzying excesses to uphold.

When the original members reunited in 2001, Warren Cuccurullo made his exit after almost fifteen years with the band. John states in his 2012 memoir (*In the Pleasure Groove: Love, Death, and Duran Duran*) that Warren's departure was by amicable mutual consent; Warren claims he was first notified of the decision to give him the boot via a letter from Simon and Nick. Tomato, tomahto. The reunited Durans recorded an album, 2003's *Astronaut*, and embarked upon a successful world tour. Nostalgic for the past, audiences welcomed them back. *Astronaut* produced a modest hit single in the cheerful anthem "(Reach Up for the) Sunrise"; there's a video for it, too, the first one made by the five original members since "A View to a Kill," in which the Durans go on separate journeys: Simon zips a motorcycle through the Pyrenees, John wanders on foot across a desert, Roger tools a vintage Jaguar past Big Ben, Andy drives a jeep around his adopted homeland of Ibiza, and Nick, ever the wildcard, flies a sparkly pink spherical spaceship over the streets of London.

Andy quit the band for the second and presumably final time in 2006. He details the events surrounding his departure at length in his entertaining 2008 memoir, *Wild Boy: My Life in Duran Duran*; there appear to have been multiple contributing factors behind the split, though he places the bulk of the blame on his personal differences with one particular band member. Hint: It's the one he refers to as a "Revlon-wearing tosser."[13]

Duran Duran's first post-Andy album, 2007's *Red Carpet Massacre*, was shaped by a handful of high-profile producers, including Justin Timberlake and hip hop artist Timbaland; the result seems fuzzy, scattershot, unfocused. There's nothing especially *wrong* with it, but it doesn't sound much like Duran Duran; it spawned no hits, and critical reaction was tepid. It did produce one slickly stylish video: In "Falling Down," directed by Anthony Mandler, the four Durans play hilariously unconvincing medical professionals at a rehab clinic populated entirely by strung out, scantily-clad models. John, still breathtakingly lovely well into middle age, solemnly doles out medication to gangly beauties in stilettos and feathered shrugs; Simon totes a clipboard while looking brainy and earnest in spectacles and a white coat. It's ridiculous and adorable.

Better still, though, is the video for "Girl Panic!", off of 2011's *All You Need Is Now* album, in which a handful of top supermodels of yore pose as the band members. Naomi Campbell is Simon, Cindy Crawford is John, Helena Christensen is Roger, Simon's wife Yasmin Le Bon is the unidentified guitarist—view her as an amalgam of Andy, Warren, and Dom Brown, who has recorded and toured with the band consistently since Andy's second departure—and Eva Herzigová steals the whole damn show as a whip-smart and malevolently shallow Nick ("I wrote the last song. I take full credit for it," Eva-as-Nick hisses at an interviewer, who is played by the real Nick. Eva *gets* Nick). Directed by Jonas Åkerlund "Girl Panic!" is a champagne-soaked, glitter-encrusted delight.

All You Need Is Now, produced by Mark Ronson and designed as a kind of spiritual successor to their famed *Rio* album, generated good reviews and good will, though its modest success has since been eclipsed by their follow-up album, *Paper Gods*, which was released in 2015; here in early 2017, Duran Duran are still touring on the strength of it. A critical darling, *Paper Gods* features a mix of solid, catchy, crowd-pleasing songs like the title track, and sundry weird shit like "Danceophobia," which contains a bizarre spoken-word part performed by Lindsay Lohan posing as a doctor. Never change, Duran Duran.

They're doing well. They're staples at art gallery openings, at Fashion Week, at awards shows and private parties. In recent years, they've performed at SXSW, at

Coachella, at Madison Square Garden. Their music pops up in ad campaigns for upscale brands: Michael Kors, Dior Addict. They are the glamorous elder statesmen of pop music, well-preserved ambassadors of a bygone era.

I've never met a Duran. I don't expect that will change. I'm still not entirely certain I believe they exist, even though I've seen them onstage a handful of times by now. Their level of celebrity makes them seem inaccessible, remote, as though they exist in a universe parallel to this one, where others can view them from afar but never interact with them. Their universe is glittery and glamorous and very, very strange. May it endure forever.

ACKNOWLEDGMENTS

NOBODY IS DESERVING of my gratitude more than my sister, Ingrid Richter, for her constant support and her benevolent tolerance—nay, encouragement—of my Duran Duran obsession. I am, as always, in her debt.

In researching this book, I was aided by a handful of kind Duranies who helped me track down some hard-to-find resources; since the bulk of our interaction has been Twitter-based, I'm going to refer to them by their Twitter handles. Special kudos to the great @allegrao for ruthlessly hunting down the source of an obscure Simon Le Bon quote I feared was lost to the ages. Thanks are also due to @csjensen68, @BoysMakeNoise, @Tin_Hotha, and @DuranDuranInfo.

Much gratitude goes out to the boundlessly good-natured Andy "Durandy" Golub for being a consummate host and opening his famed and fabulous Duran Duran archive to me. Thank you as well to Melissa Joulwan for generously giving me her prized collection of Duran Duran tour books, and to Andy Taylor for being a good sport about reposting some of my early Duranalyses on his official site back in 2012, despite all the uncharitable jokes I've made about his hair over the years.

And thank you, of course, to Duran Duran for decades of glamour, inspiration, and entertainment. May we have many, many more years of this.

ABOUT THE AUTHOR

MORGAN RICHTER IS the author of nine books, including *Bias Cut*, a 2012 semifinalist for the Amazon Breakthrough Novel Award (ABNA) and a silver medalist at the 2013 Independent Publisher Book Awards. She has worked in production on television shows such as *Talk Soup* and *America's Funniest Home Videos*, and has contributed pop culture reviews to websites such as TVgasm and Forces of Geek, as well as to her own site, Preppies of the Apocalypse. Born in Spokane, Washington, she currently lives in New York City.

BIBLIOGRAPHY

[1] Taylor, John, and Tom Sykes. *In the Pleasure Groove: Love, Death, & Duran Duran.* New York, New York: Penguin Group Inc., 2012

[2] *Duran Duran: The Book of Words.* Edited by De Graaf Garrett. Winona, Minnesota: Hal Leonard Publishing Corporation, 1984

[3] Taylor, John, and Tom Sykes. *In the Pleasure Groove: Love, Death, & Duran Duran.* New York, New York: Penguin Group Inc., 2012

[4] Johnson, Richard. "Five Go F***ing Mad in Whitley Bay," *The Sunday Times*, February 18, 1996

[5] Hickey, Walt. "Men are sabotaging the online reviews of TV shows aimed at women," FiveThirtyEight.com, May 18, 2016

[6] "Interview with Simon Le Bon and Roger Taylor," *BBC Radio Five Live.* BBC Radio Five, June 13, 2012

[7] Tannenbaum, Rob, and Craig Marks. *I Want My MTV: The Uncensored Story of the Music Video Revolution*. New York, New York: Penguin Group, Inc., 2011

[8] Chamberlain, Vassi, "Who's a Pretty Boy, Then?" *Tatler*, June 2003

[9] Gaiman, Neil. *Duran Duran: The First Four Years of the Fab Five*. London, England: Proteus Publishing Group, 1984

[10] Green, Michelle, "A Madcap Video Shoot in Paris Yields a View to Kill For: The Five Faces of Duran Duran." *People Magazine*, July 22, 1985

[11] Russell Powell, Fiona, "Andy Warhol: The Face Interview." *The Face*, March 1985

[12] "Canadians Give Duran Duran the Cold Shoulder." *MTV News*, November 10, 1997

[13] Taylor, Andy. *Wild Boy: My Life in Duran Duran*. New York, New York: Grand Central Publishing, 2008.

Printed in Great Britain
by Amazon

14541257R00079